DATE DUE

-60

1. Indians of North America—Biography.
I. T.

CANADIAN PORTRAITS

FAMOUS INDIANS

Canadian Portraits

Brant Crowfoot Oronhyatekha
FAMOUS INDIANS

By

Ethel Brant Monture

CLARKE, IRWIN & COMPANY LIMITED
Toronto   1960   Vancouver

COPYRIGHT, CANADA, 1960
by CLARKE, IRWIN & COMPANY LIMITED

First printed,	*May, 1960*
Reprinted,	*June, 1962*
Reprinted,	*October, 1966*
Reprinted,	*January, 1970*

Printed in Canada

CONTENTS

v

ILLUSTRATIONS

vii

THAYENDANEGEA

Joseph Brant

THAYENDANEGEA

Joseph Brant

THROUGH the years many historians have written of Joseph Brant, either as Joseph Brant or as Thayendanegea, as he was called by the Mohawks. Some of these writers have presented a legendary figure, an Indian, a scalper and a fiend: one such story about him was entitled "Thayendanegea, Scourge of the Mohawks". Others have made him a tragic and pitiful figure trying to stem an incoming tide that overwhelmed his people in their homeland. His own people like to think of him as a capable leader maintaining their tradition of social responsibility, for he shared their hardships in a time of disaster and upheaval when he might have taken an easier road, and he found the way for them to a settled and dignified life again.

The Indians were by no means primitive nomads at the time of the Europeans' arrival. As Thomas R. Henry remarks: "When the white man came a great Indian culture was flourishing in the wilderness of what is now New York State."[1] This confederacy has been called "one of the few pure republics the world

[1] *Wilderness Messiah*, William Sloane Associates, 1955.

had known"; and anthropologists say it was "an amazing development in political theory". Its beginnings go back to the middle of the fifteenth century. The principles laid down by Dekanawida, a statesman of the Indians in that early time, were the foundation of a government of the people by the people, for authority then flowed upward from the family unit or fireside, with men and women having equal responsibility.

The men were first of all hunters and warriors whose skill in battle strategy later influenced the military techniques of the Old World armies. Indians had also learned to battle their ills with medicines of their own discovery obtained from the native plants and trees, and with surgery and psychiatry, as well as with magic and religion, so that every tribe had members with particular ability to heal—their medicine men. And the men were also the councillors and lawmakers, but they were chosen and appointed by the women.

Neither sex felt superior or inferior. Women had the special honour of growing the food from the land because it was a tribal belief that the Mother Earth gave them all life. One of the oldest laws of the Confederacy was, "Woman, the mother, shall have care of all that is planted by which life is sustained and supported. Woman has been endowed with high honour and with full measure of mind and reason." Men prepared for the planting by clearing

4

the land but the cornfields belonged to the women. Corn, they believed, was a maiden to be cared for only by women.

The Confederacy was composed of five tribes: the Mohawks, the Onondagas and the Senecas were the senior tribes and the Oneidas and Cayugas were the younger brothers. Its symbol was a tall pine tree, said to be growing from a soil composed of the good principles of health of body, sanity of mind, right conduct in thought and deed, justice for each one, a sense of spiritual life and a right to self-defence. They called this their "Tree of Peace", and they came to call themselves the "People of the Longhouse", for their homeland, which later became New York State, they likened to their dwellings, which were long bark structures each sheltering several related families. The Confederacy with its tribal families extended from the Hudson River in the east to Niagara in the west. The Mohawks in their beloved valley were called the "Keepers of the Eastern Door", while the Senecas of the Genesee and Niagara watched the door in the west. The Onondagas were the "Keepers of the Fire".

The Confederacy had grown powerful for the tribes had built a good trading system based on hunting and on agricultural development. They also had transportation facilities, so that first the Dutch and later the English eagerly sought an alliance with them. The colonies of England grew slowly from feeble youth to sturdy manhood, shielded from aggression by the League of the Five Nations. In the early years of the eighteenth century the tribes of the Tuscaroras, after much conflict with the settlers on their lands in the Carolinas, asked for admission to the Confederacy. Thereafter it was known as the Six Nations.

The prized hunting lands of the Six Nations, or, as they were also called, the Iroquois, were in what is now the state of Ohio. It was the custom to station hunters there to protect them from invasion and to keep a supply of meat and skins for food and clothing flowing back to the homeland. Many adventurous couples in their early married life went there to spend a few years before settling down in the tribal lands in New York State. Joseph Brant's young parents were in Ohio when his sister Molly was born in 1737 and they were still there in 1742 when he was born. His mother told him years later that when she performed the birth rite of washing her newborn son in the nearest running water it was the Muskingum River and the water was full of leaping ice. So Joseph knew he was born in the spring. And he always contended that this icy baptism was what made him strong.

His family returned to the Mohawk Valley when he was eight years old to find that many more Europeans had settled there. His people were influential and his mother had duties to assume, for she

6

would now belong to the Society of Matrons who chose the sachems for the council. Joseph owed much to his wise mother; in her comfortable home he became accustomed to mingling with the people of the two races now living in their beloved valley.

Little Joseph did not have an idle childhood; an Indian boy in those days had to start at an early age to learn the skills that would make him a hunter and a warrior, and on which his life would depend. He also had to learn to speak well for later he might be chosen for the councils. Hendrick, the wise and eloquent head chief of the Mohawks, was Joseph's boyhood ideal; he never tired of listening to his deep voice in the councils. Hendrick had been the leader of the Confederacy at the Albany Congress of 1754, when delegates of the thirteen English colonies met to form some sort of union for mutual protection. The Indian tribes in New England, antagonized by the land-snatching of the colonists, were always on the alert for opportunities to make reprisals on them; and the French also had dreams of an empire in the New World and resented the Iroquois-English alliance which turned the fur trade they coveted towards English markets. This double threat brought the colonists together, although they were still divided among themselves over who should lead them. One of the delegates, Benjamin Franklin, had gone to a council of the Confederacy, and, like some earlier observers, he saw the strength in the union of Indian nations which had "one head, one mind, one body and one life". He told the delegates to the convention that they would do well to form an alliance of the same pattern, saying, "It would be a strange thing if Six Nations of ignorant savages should be capable of forming a scheme for such a union and able to execute it in such a manner that it has subsisted for ages and appears indissoluble; and yet that a like union should be impracticable for ten or a dozen English colonies to whom it is more necessary and must be more advantageous to their interests." Such a political organization was new to the minds of the colonists, but after many weeks they adopted the Indian confederacy pattern because they could think of nothing better.

For a long time now the Six Nations had been sharing their New York State homelands with many newcomers from Europe. These newcomers also shared the food supplies and the trap lines of the land, depleting its resources, since it took ten square miles of hunting territory to keep a family in food. The growing uneasiness of the Six Nations under these circumstances is understandable. The Mohawk villages now were frontier towns. This made life increasingly difficult, for the natives had their many ceremonials and festivals which were vital to their living but were misunderstood and looked upon as heathen by the crowding settlers. At the Niagara door of the Longhouse, the Senecas, far

8

from contact with the settlers, sometimes twitted the Mohawks with being more European than Indian. This did not please the Mohawks, for they found the ever-crowding settlers irksome, hectoring and stupid.

These incoming settlers brought their wars, religions, rum and gunpowder from Europe with them, as well as their devastating epidemics and diseases. These diseases were new to America; the medicine men had no remedies for them, and they swept over the Indian folk like a killing wind. Whole villages died of the smallpox. The Indians believed the settlers carried these diseases in their breaths and, especially after an outbreak, they feared contact with any of them, even the priests. The Mohawks held long council meetings trying to find some solution. Most of the settlers had taken up residence in their homelands and they were being elbowed out. They suffered most from the new sicknesses; it was a blow to them when young warriors died, many of them before they left children to grow in their places. A few of their young women had been taken as wives by the Dutch and the English. They did not approve of this because the children of these marriages would be lost to the Indians when the great need was to keep the tribes strong.

Another troublesome subject was the land. The oldest Indian belief was that the land was the Earth Mother free for all and possessed by none. They had no concept of individual land titles and so were

9

not very much perturbed when a newcomer told them in council that the English king had given a wide stretch of their land to pay a debt to one of his soldiers who had won a victory for him. The king was far away. Their land was free to all for hunting, as free as the air for breathing, and they loved it as a mother.

At first, the Europeans had begun their New World enterprises as trading companies chartered by their rulers, who wanted fresh sources of revenue. Settlement came later. The Dutch, who came first, were unconcerned with any plans other than selling their goods and getting a profitable return in furs. Then the English came, rooted out the Dutch and took over their trade.

The French approach to the Mohawk Valley had been by way of Canada. The first French colonists learned to be canoemen and set off with the Indian fur brigades to trade and explore. Their priests became missionaries, eager to convert the Indians. Father Paul Le Jeune, in the now collected writings of these early priests, the Jesuit *Relations*, recorded this: "I have scarcely seen one person who came to this country from France who does not acknowledge the Indians have more intellect and capacity than most of our peasants." Yet there was not much friendliness between the French and the People of the Longhouse because of a foolish caprice of Champlain, who had wished to impress the Indians he had met with the power of the French. The ghost of his ill-considered action forever haunted the French.

Samuel de Champlain in 1609 was the manager of the French Company's depot at Quebec. He was an excellent fur-trader; by fair dealing he had built friendly trading connections with the Montagnais nearby as well as with the Hurons from the west. For years the Mohawks had been the middlemen who bought from many tribes in the west and carried the fur cargoes down their own river to resell them to the Dutch and later to the English in Albany. The French had interrupted this fur stream, hoping to divert it into the St. Lawrence River for French profit. The Mohawks retaliated by ambushing the cargoes on the way to Lachine and the French depot.

Champlain saw it as a duty to put a stop to this. He took a war party of French, Montagnais and Hurons, the French armed with harquebuses. The party attacked a camp of the Mohawks on the eastern shore of the lake now called Lake Champlain. Champlain thus described the event: "The enemy, about two hundred, left their barricade and came toward us. They were preparing to shoot their arrows at us. I raised my harquebus, which had four balls in it, aiming directly at the chief and fired. Two of them fell dead and one other was wounded. They were greatly surprised at seeing their men killed so suddenly, notwithstanding they were provided with arrow-proof armour. While I was reloading my companions fired which so astonished them, that seeing their leaders slain, they lost courage and I pursued them and killed some others." He went on to relate how the French were greatly amused at the astonishment of the Mohawks when they saw guns fired. This was a costly and unfortunate victory: Champlain had antagonized the People of the Longhouse; they never trusted the French again.

To make matters worse, Louis XIV of France sent this directive to the French in the New World in 1684: "As it tends to the good of my servants to diminish the number of the Iroquois and as they are very strong and robust they will serve usefully in my galleys, I will that you do everything in your power to make a great number of prisoners of war and at every opportunity have them conveyed to France." To make the order attractive, ten *écus* were offered for every Iroquois killed, with twice as much for each prisoner. No wonder relations between the French and the Iroquois never mended! The warriors of the Confederacy knew that some of their brothers were pulling oars on French galleys, and when they captured a French prisoner they took revenge. Moreover, a horrible epidemic had attacked them shortly after a French priest had arrived in their lands. Many died of it and this they also laid to the charge of the French.

The bitterness of the People of the Longhouse toward the French suited the English. In 1664 they made a treaty with the Iroquois at Albany signed by four Mohawks, two Senecas, one Onondaga and one Cayuga, all chiefs of the Confederacy. This treaty secured the English colonies. Governor Dongan triumphantly reported: "The Five Nations are a bulwark between us and the French and all other Indians."

Most of the early immigrants were the landless and poor of their own countries. The vast stretches of the New World forests and the mighty rivers and lakes awed them until they became obsessed with dreams of ownership in the feudal style that was traditional in Europe. Even those born at the bottom of the social scale could hope to see such dreams realized. They resented the Indians, who stood between them and the land they coveted.

One day a man arrived who said he was to live on the land of his uncle, an admiral in the British navy whom the English king had paid for a sea victory by giving him land in the Mohawk country. The newcomer was an Irishman named William Johnson. Later, when he became a trader, the Mohawks grew to like him, for his heart was honest and he was strong and pleasant on a hard hunt. When they knew him well they liked him more and more because he never pried into their lives. Much later they gave this Irishman a Mohawk name, Warraghiyagey, which meant simply "Man of Business", and he never dishonoured it; he pleased the whole Confederacy.

Soon after coming to the Mohawk country William Johnson took as wife Catherine Weisenberg, a German immigrant girl, but she died early and left him with two small daughters and a son. He then asked the Mohawks to allow him to marry beautiful Caroline, the niece of Hendrick, their head chief. Caroline was the daughter of Abraham, also a chief, whose second wife had been a Dutch woman. The Mohawks consented to the marriage because Johnson had won the respect of the whole Confederacy. He made no pretence to superiority and he kept sacred his promises. William Johnson was proud of his wife but he was preoccupied with his business. The English government highly approved of his friendship with the Confederacy and he was expected to hold its good will. His dream, like that of many others, was to acquire wide lands and prestige. He built a fine new house near his trading post on the Mohawk River and called it Fort Johnson; and he won an appointment as Justice of the Peace.

Pretty Caroline died when her children, two girls and a boy, were still infants. The son was named William for his father but he lived at the Mohawk village of Canajoharie with his grandfather, Chief Abraham. When Joseph Brant's parents returned to their Mohawk home from Ohio, six-year-old William Johnson was two years younger than Joseph.

14

A friendship grew between them that was to last all their lives; they became indeed brothers.

While Joseph was being disciplined for life, his mother had sent his sister Molly, five years his senior, to a school for young ladies at nearby Schenectady. She had learned from her mother all the domestic arts of an Indian woman, such as how to beat a deerskin to a velvety softness, and how to be deft in sewing. She was sometimes wilful but never malicious. Her years at the young ladies' school with Dutch and English girls were happy, and when she came back to her home in the Mohawk village she brought books to teach the girls there what she had learned. She was a willing learner.

William Johnson saw her and for the second time he asked the Mohawk Council for one of their daughters. This did not please them. Caroline had lived for such a short time as his wife and now her children were motherless. Moreover it had been their hope that Molly would soon marry one of their own people, for she gave promise that in the years to come she would be much like her mother and such fine women could not be spared from the tribe. But William Johnson was still the friend who never criticized their ways or broke their laws and so, reluctantly, they let the wedding arrangements be made.

Molly had no awe of the handsome house that would be her home. Because William Johnson was the king's representative, he was expected to wel-

come the great and the small who came his way.
Molly became known as a hostess of unusual grace
and social wisdom; her husband grew increasingly
proud of her. And their door was always open to
her people.

Honours were thrust upon William Johnson. He
did not aspire to be a military man but still saw
himself as a landed gentleman such as he had known
in his youth in Ireland. Yet he was given a general's
commission in the Army as well as an appointment
as "His Majesty's Sole Agent for all affairs to the Six
Nations and other Northern Indians". This last
duty was the more agreeable to him.

The Mohawks' one criticism of William Johnson
was of his endless appetite for land. Hendrick, the
leader of the Mohawks at the battle of Lake George,
recounted how he once met William Johnson after
the latter became a general. He admired the handsome red coat the General was wearing, and, because
he loved a joke, he slyly told William Johnson that
he had dreamed that Johnson had once given him
such a coat. Johnson stripped off the coat and gave
it to Hendrick on the spot. A few days later, Johnson met Hendrick again and told him that he too
had dreamed: he had dreamed that the Mohawks
had given him a wide stretch of land he had long
coveted. Hendrick saw he had been tricked, but
the Mohawks agreed to give the land, although
Hendrick made Johnson promise to dream no more.

And so, affected by the dreams of William Johnson and many less kindly and less respectful men, Joseph's people saw a new way of life taking hold in their lands. His mother studied the changes and knew that children would need more than the usual rigorous training of Indian youth. A settlers' school had been started in the village of Canajoharie, where reading and writing were taught. Here Joseph was sent to study, but he was a reluctant pupil: their beloved river, the Mohawk, a busy water-road, was a sore temptation to any school boy. Later he went to a school for Indian children at Fort Hunter. The medicine man who trained the boys of the Mohawks to be cunning hunters and hardy warriors did not relax his programme because of the schools: the boys had to sit quietly and listen to the men in the councils. Frequently they were taken far into the hills and each left alone to live off the land and find the way home. The medicine man said this made them know themselves.

Joseph grew strong and hardy. At thirteen he was thin but tall and wiry, toughened by his Spartan training. He shared the Mohawks' fondness for festivals and dances. They were a gay people; indeed, the French priests complained that they were too much so.

The English and the French were always ready to battle each other and in 1755 a conflict broke out between them in North America on Confederacy and Mohawk lands. William Johnson, now General, was ordered to capture the French Fort Carillon on Lake Champlain. The French had dared to build forts on Indian lands, saying they were for trade.

For all their gaiety, war was a part of life with the People of the Longhouse; their young men were hardened for it. They thought that a people was soon like a dead tree without such hardening; besides, war was a clean and a good way for death to take those who were weak. A people must be kept strong. Moreover the new general, William Johnson, was like one of themselves. If he was trying to drive the French from their land this was their war. The Mohawks, Onondagas and Oneidas joined Johnson's force with Hendrick as their leader. They were all given new guns. Since the days of Champlain and his "firesticks", all Indians had acquired guns. They did not use them much for hunting because the older men maintained it was wiser to kill their food with their own weapons. But in a war the best arrows were weak before guns. Like the new diseases, guns slew too many hunters and warriors.

Joseph, at thirteen, was tall enough to go with the warriors. The first ordeal and, Joseph thought, the worst, was having the hair on each side of his head plucked to a roach or scalp-lock such as all the Mohawk warriors wore. But he revelled in the excitement of war-making.

They met the French, under Baron Ludwig

August Dieskau, at Lake George. The British suffered, at first, from their ignorance of forest warfare, but after they had lost a thousand men they were ready to listen to William Johnson when he told them to build a barricade of logs and brush. This abattis held against the French and the highly trained French soldiers fell back. The French general had been contemptuous of the provincial British troops, but they prevailed over his white-uniformed regiment and the Baron himself was wounded and captured. General William Johnson received a wound that was to trouble him for the rest of his life.

Joseph later told his sister Molly that when the noise of battle began he was so frightened that he had to hold on to a tree to keep from running away. But now he was counted as a warrior. Now, too, the first sorrow had come into his life: all the Confederacy mourned because Hendrick, his hero and the Confederacy's leader, had been killed at Lake George with many other warriors.

Joseph went back to the school at Fort Hunter but maturity was thrust upon him in 1757 when John Campbell, Earl of Loudon, Commander-in-Chief of the British forces in America, gave him a commission as a captain in His Majesty's Royal American Regiment. Lord Loudon had received orders from England to pay particular attention to the Iroquois, and later the King personally gave him the order to hold them as allies. The Seven Years' War had broken out in 1756 and a fierce battle between those ancient enemies, the French and the English, took place at Niagara in 1759. This resulted in a British victory, which broke the line of French forts between the St. Lawrence and Louisiana. The British were helped in this battle by many Senecas, Keepers of the Western Door of the Longhouse, under a new war leader named Sangerachta; and they took full part now, for the battlefield was in their own lands. They, too, wanted to be freed from the intruders.

General William Johnson, who for his victory over the French at Lake George had been made a baronet, was not as close to the Senecas as to the Mohawks; he had to prove himself in their eyes. Winning this frontier battle was the test. Here Joseph, taller and still sapling-thin, in his new dignity as a British officer with Indian embellishments and Mohawk scalp-lock, was the victim of much good-natured banter. He enjoyed it, though, for he knew men did not look on him as a small boy any longer but as an equal. He felt that life was good.

After the battle at Niagara, Joseph was the hunter for his family. He spent long days in the hills, often alone, sometimes with the young William Johnson. Back in the Mohawk homelands he pondered many things: his people were tired of war; they mourned for their sons. He had often heard from the story-teller the history of their ancient Confederacy established to promote peace. Peace did not

[FACING: *Joseph, in his new dignity as a British officer with Indian embellishments and Mohawk scalp-lock, led his men in a fierce battle at Niagara in 1759.*

grow easily and there was no peace in the valley now.

His grandfathers' concept that the land was as free for everyone as the air one breathed had changed in the last generation: from a generous sharing the Indians passed to a jealous guardianship of the land as they saw squatters' cabins spring up like morels in the valley. Soon the squatters were disputing the Indians' right to travel their deep-trodden trails across their own lands. Unless steps were taken to defend their rights the people of the Confederacy might suffer the misfortunes endured by the New England tribes at the hands of the settlers there.

In New Hampshire, at Lebanon, a school called Moor's Indian Charity School was asking for students. The schoolmaster, the Reverend Eleazer Wheelock, boasted that he could "make Christian Englishmen out of red heathen". The Council decided that those who chose to go should do so, not to be changed to Englishmen but because some of the young warriors should know the new ways. About twenty young men of the Longhouse, including Joseph and young William Johnson, went to Lebanon. They enjoyed school life. They could be friendly with the Reverend Wheelock, whom they thought honest, though sometimes tiresomely boastful. At home, in fact, his ways would be considered bad manners. Samuel Kirkland, a New England youth who much later became a Congregational missionary to the Oneidas, was a fellow student.

Still the war kettle simmered. Pontiac, leader of the Ottawas, a tribe in the Lake Huron country which had been the ally of the French, saw that the English and French called his people "friends" only when they needed help in a battle. He told a great council of western Indians that this fighting was not for the sake of the Indians: the English and French wanted Indian lands for themselves. The council listened eagerly when he asked them to hold together as one people to drive all white people out of the land forever. Delegations were sent to distant tribes to ask them to join. One such deputation came to the People of the Longhouse. They held a long council. The Senecas were angry with the English over a recent encroachment on their rights at a portage at Niagara which they had held for a long time. The English had appropriated it for themselves. One old Onondaga sachem had never agreed that the Indians join either French or English as allies. His words, "Let the white men fight each other till all are killed. Then we will have our land free again," were generally ignored. A party of angry young Senecas decided to join Pontiac. Their decision was hard for the Confederacy Council to accept; yet the Senecas' right to make the decision had to be conceded. But it was a grief that Confederacy warriors were on both sides.

The Mohawks, pinched territorially with the

many settlers about them, and hampered in their trading as they were, knew they had a treaty with the English. Treaties were sacred promises. So, when General Sir William Johnson was ordered to take troops to Detroit, the Longhouse warriors, mostly Mohawks, went with him. The young men came back from the Wheelock school. All the young men who had been away at school had made sure of not letting themselves get soft, for if their old trainer had not approved of them they would have been ridiculed by their people. Under the spur of public opinion they had boxed and wrestled strenuously for exercise between sessions of Latin and Bible study. Joseph needed a new uniform.

All this time the French, to gain what they might from Pontiac's plan, talked vaguely of guns that would come from the French king to help him; but the guns did not come and Pontiac did not expect them. Even without them his plan to regain his country almost worked.

The British officer in charge of Fort Detroit, the British trading centre and supply base, refused to believe an invasion by Pontiac was imminent. Catherine, a girl of the Ojibways, allies of Pontiac, who had as one writer states won the favour of the British officer, brought him word that the invasion would begin when a party of Pontiac's men, all carrying concealed guns, would come to trade. The officer listened to her and when the advance party arrived they found all the soldiers inside the fort carrying their guns openly. Pontiac's men therefore did not attack, but this was the beginning of a siege that lasted for months. Detroit and Fort Pitt were the two forts to hold out while one post after another went down. At last it was impossible for Pontiac to obtain guns or gunpowder and he was compelled to admit defeat.

Historians have been reluctant to admit that the timely warning of Catherine saved the fort. Romantic writers have said she gave the alarm because she was in love with the British officer. The fact remains that the women of Pontiac's Ottawas and of the Ojibways, his Huron allies, did not like war any more than women of any other race. Catherine knew that many men had been killed and more would be, and she dared to interfere and save them.

A treaty was made at Fort Stanwix. General Johnson knew there had to be some definite promises from the English. At a grand council attended by delegates from many Indian tribes, a border line called the Stanwix Line was set. Traders were forbidden to come and go as they pleased; all must have a registered licence and there was to be a fair price for furs, openly posted. It took months for the war excitement to die down.

After Sir William Johnson finally got back to his home at Johnstown, he hoped only that he might be able to stay there. While he had been at the wars,

Molly, his beloved wife, had kept the charming home, watching over the children and their education, for there was now a school where Johnson's children and the children of his tenants spent their days. Now Sir William could realize his dream of living in the style of an English baron and make a good life for himself in the valley he had come to love well. He also brought a nephew, Guy Johnson, from Ireland, who came, as he himself had come, a penniless youth to make a living in the New World. He tried hard to train this nephew Guy to take over some of his heavy burden of work, with not very much success. His eldest son, John, did not seem ready to assume any responsibility and his father liked to have him live as the privileged son of a wealthy landowner.

Sir William sorely needed an interpreter and an aide in his Indian business. This was an enviable post, because of Sir William's respected position. Although many young men presented themselves, Sir William chose Brant as the most trustworthy. Brant agreed and left the Wheelock school, for good this time, much to the sorrow of the schoolmaster who had thought he might make a good missionary of him. The new job paid Joseph eighty-three pounds a year and travelling expenses. He lived part of the year at Johnson Hall where he met the many visitors who came on business or to while away a vacation, and he learned to like Sir William's way of life. There was also a singular devotion be-

tween him and his sister Molly, whose competence he
never ceased to admire.

Joseph enjoyed his work as Sir William's business
agent. After the quiet of the Wheelock school the
tumult of this frontier life shook away his *naïveté*
and taught him to study men. He ran into opposition from some of the traders who complained that
he showed too much partiality to his own people.
For instance, he knew that a certain trading company was buying old discarded guns from the Army,
filling the cracks in the barrels with molten lead, and
reselling the weapons to young Indians. At the first
firing the guns exploded, often maiming a hunter's
hands. When Joseph proved this in court, the trading company's licence was revoked. The men involved became Joseph's active enemies but their
plan to have him assassinated backfired. The feud
went on for years, with occasional ambushes and
pitched battles though without much hurt to anyone. One of the traders, Ezra Buell, admitted in
his old age that he had kept up a campaign of
rumour and slander against Joseph for years until
the Mohawks left the valley.

Joseph was now in a position where he could
choose a wife. It was not the custom for the young
men to marry until they had made their mark. So,
forthwith his people prepared for his wedding to
Christine, the daughter of Sauquoit, or Antonc as
the Dutch at Albany called him, a chief of the

Oneidas and their interpreter. Christine and Joseph had known each other when they were pupils in the Fort Hunter school. Besides the customary tribal celebrations they had an Anglican wedding ceremony. They decided to live near the church lately built on the south side of the Mohawk River, where Joseph had a farm inherited from Hendrick. History mentions Christine only in passing. Once Joseph accompanied a traveller, Richard Smith, who wished to be shown the Susquehanna River, and he took his wife and small son Isaac in the canoe with them. The traveller wrote later that a double row of Indian brooches trimmed her skirt beautifully. The Reverend John Stuart of Fort Hunter, who had been their schoolmaster, wrote in 1771: "On my first visit to the village of Canajoharie, 30 miles west of Fort Hunter, Brant had a good house with everything necessary for the use of his family. His wife was in the last stages of consumption [tuberculosis] and died soon after leaving him with two little children, his beloved son Isaac and a daughter Christine." It was in this troubled time that Joseph spent many days with Mr. Stuart; they worked together on a translation into the Mohawk language of the Acts of the Apostles.

In 1773 Joseph asked Mr. Stuart to marry him again, to Susannah, his sister-in-law. He explained that because she was closely related she would take good care of his children whenever he had to leave

28

them. Mr. Stuart refused, because of church laws forbidding a man to marry his deceased wife's sister, and Joseph went to a German Lutheran who did as he asked. This marriage lasted a very short time, for Susannah died within a few months. There was no help for any person who had consumption.

In these years land troubles increased. Halsey, a writer of the period, said, "Since the conclusion of the Fort Stanwix Treaty, which set a boundary between the settlers and the Indians, there had been chronic trouble over lands around the Mohawk villages." Joseph was called to many places to settle land matters. And Sir William sometimes had difficulty explaining some of the transactions: it seemed that his great appetite for land was not yet satisfied.

Joseph's most arduous duty was the regulation of trade, especially as the adventurous souls who were the bulk of the traders desired no supervision of their dealings. To acquire lands was their chief aim. The commandants of the posts asked for more soldiers to help protect Indian lands, but soon the soldiers joined the land-seekers.

In July 1774, the whole of the Longhouse as well as delegates from western tribes gathered at Johnson Hall to hear Sir William explain British trade policy for the future. Most of the faces before him were cold and unsmiling. As he talked, a heart attack seized him and he could not be revived. His last words were to Joseph Brant: "Joseph, control your people." Because Molly was heartbroken and because Sir William was an adopted Mohawk, the sachems forgot they had come to question him. After the church and Masonic services, the solemn rites of the Condolence Council of the Confederacy ended with the laying of a belt of six strings of black wampum on the grave of Warraghiyageh, William Johnson.

This was only one of their sorrows. For many months a heaviness had hung over the villages. The maple festival to mark the end of winter had lasted for only a day and the ceremony of the strawberry first fruits and the usually happy corn-planting had passed almost unnoticed, although the women had dried the fruit and planted much corn.

The truth was, the League was having difficulty holding together, pulled as it was in opposite ways, chiefly by differences between the tribes in their relations with the incoming settlers. The sachems and the warriors held long councils but there was little they could do. The laws of the League gave each tribe full power over its own affairs and the Oneidas had chosen to withdraw themselves from the Confederacy. A few Oneidas had come to the last Grand Council, evasive and sullen. They had refused to take their accustomed place between the Onondagas and the Mohawks and had gone away. The Oneidas had been separated from the League by their New England missionary, Kirkland. They had not sought

Kirkland but he had come to them and they had not turned him away. He had no understanding of an alliance such as their Confederacy and his religion, which they had accepted, taught that everything Indian was heathen. They did not know that the back of his sermon paper was covered with land measurements. He had persuaded them to ally them-selves with the rebellious colonists whose protests against British rule were soon to lead to the Ameri-can Revolution. Before leaving the Council, they had laughed at the Mohawks, saying that the Mo-hawks' treaty with the British would burn them up like weeds in a cornfield.

The sachems from the other tribes could have drawn together the Confederacy, shutting out the Oneidas, but that was not the way of kindness. The door of the Longhouse was forever open. The war-riors pitied the reluctance of the sachems to admit that the Tree of Peace could decay.

The Mohawks had long heard the seditious talk of the New England settlers around them and knew their reasons for turning against the British govern-ment. The settlers' talk of freedom struck a deep note of understanding, for the people of the League had had independence. Now, as in a nightmare, they seemed to have lost it. Sir William, in his last days, had blamed the Bostonians for what he called "these damnable heresies", and, like him, many of his old neighbours were steadfast in their loyalty to

England. Joseph understood Sir William's last request to control his people as an admonition to be loyal to the British cause. But there was no thought of change among the Mohawks for they all remembered that they had a treaty with the Brtitish.

The Tuscaroras were not ready to talk of wars, but a few of them were joining the rebels, with the Oneidas. The Onondagas had been devastated by a crippling epidemic of smallpox. The hearts of the Senecas were with the British, although they and the Cayugas were far from the scene.

In the 1770's there was great unease and uncertainty everywhere. The leaders of the American Revolution asked the Mohawks to remain neutral but would give no guarantee that their lands would be secure. Some of the settlers had become arrogant, often coming boldly to Indian homes as if they already owned them. The settlers had long been irked by the open contempt of the Mohawk sachems, who considered them without manners or dignity. In return, the settlers lost no opportunity to belittle the Indians. After Johnson's death the sachems of the Confederacy were like men in a trance. Never before had they been so helpless. Their ancient treaty had become a trap, for they were forced to wait for leadership. Joseph continued as Indian Agent when Guy Johnson was appointed Deputy Superintendent of Northern Indians. Guy was a drunkard, pompous, averse to any work and so

32

always at loggerheads with his superiors. Frequent word came of British defeats and, with the news that the rebels had captured the gunpowder sent from Albany for the Indians, Joseph told Guy Johnson the Council had decided that the Mohawks would all leave the valley, for they could not be defenceless. Joseph said they had planned to hold a Confederacy council of the four tribes left at Onondaga, and they would take all the women and children since they knew they would never come back. Though it was the time for the festival of thankfulness for the new corn, no festivity would take place. The valley Loyalists, as well as Superintendent Guy and Sir John Johnson, were being harried continuously by the rebel settlers and they quickly decided they too would go to Montreal, joining the Mohawks at Onondaga. This rigorous march took several weeks, and Guy Johnson's wife died on the way. Sir Guy Carleton, Governor of Canada, who met them at Montreal, praised them for leaving their homes because of their loyalty; but he had to be reminded by the Mohawks that they needed soil to put down new roots. Gunpowder for hunting food was their first great need. To earn it from the British they ambushed the Americans who were attacking St. Johns.

Joseph and the rest of the Mohawks came to the conclusion that they must know whether the British would or would not help them recover their lands. Since no one at Montreal could tell them, Sir Guy

33

Carleton arranged for Joseph to go to England with John Deseronto, his cousin. Their arrival in London in the summer of 1776 was greeted by James Boswell with this note in his journal: "The present unhappy civil war has occasioned Brant coming over to England. His manners are gentle and quiet. He had promised to put three thousand men in the field." So the Mohawks' need for lands and roofs over their heads was regarded by at least one Englishman as no more than an advantage in a British military campaign.

Lord Jeffrey Amherst, who had been commander-in-chief of the British forces in America, gave a great dinner in Joseph's honour. In his toast Amherst referred to Joseph as "His Majesty's greatest American subject". Charles James Fox, the statesman and orator, was asked to speak, but he begged Joseph to respond for himself. Joseph was reluctant, saying, "His Majesty has a good many great American subjects—some of whom," he added with a flash of a smile, "are greater than they are good!" Still referring to Amherst's personal tribute, he continued, "If the toast referred only to Indians I cannot agree, for I am here only because of some advantages for at home there are many more worthy. Among my people in my Mohawk tongue they do not care to hear me speak, and they are right, for they can listen to orators like the venerable Onnasadega of the Onondagas, or to Red Jacket, the young wonder of the Senecas, or a dozen others.

"Among the Indians there are two roads to greatness. One is the warpath, the other is the council. The council road is the most famous because fewest are able to travel on it. Almost any Indian can be a warrior. That is all I am or ever have been. Even in that I have never been anything but a subordinate under warriors much greater than I can ever hope to be, such as Hiakatoo of the Senecas or King Hendrick whose fame you all know."

Then Joseph asked permission to propose another toast, "To the memory of the greatest American subject His Majesty ever had—Sir William Johnson". The men drank the toast standing in silence.

The guests embarrassed Joseph with praises, assuring him that whether or not his own people considered him an orator he certainly was one in England.

The King gave him two audiences. The first was informal and took place at Kew Gardens; here the King presented Joseph with a pair of fine pistols, saying he wished him to wear them whenever duty called him to the warpath but never to use them against the giver or his friends. The second audience was recorded in the Court Journal. "The sachem of the Iroquois of North America was presented to His Majesty and the Queen by the Secretary of State for War. His Majesty graciously greeted the great sachem and inquired after the health of himself and his family. The sachem kissed her Majesty's hand."

Joseph attended a theatre party at the Drury

Lane Theatre to witness a performance of *Romeo and Juliet*. The Lady Ossory, a member of a famous Irish family, watched Joseph with amusement and asked him, "What do you think of that kind of love-making, Captain Brant?" Joseph retorted, "There is too much of it, your ladyship." "Why do you say that?" said the lady, and Joseph answered quickly, "Because, your ladyship, no lover worth a lady's while would waste his time and breath in all that speech-making. If my people were to make love that way our race would be extinct in two generations."

At the request of the Duke of Warwick he sat for Romney, the noted portrait artist of the day. And the Duke of Northumberland invited Joseph and his party to his country house to escape a London heat wave.

After long talks with Lord North and state officials, who wished to discuss possibilities of investment in America rather than Indian lands, he was given assurance that Indian help in the coming war would be repaid with new lands.

The *Universal Magazine* reported in London in July 1776, "The great Iroquois sachem Brant or Thayendanega embarked for America in one of His Majesty's ships at Portsmouth, May 30 last."

An old friend, Thomas Pownall, who had at an earlier time represented the British Lords of Trade in America, staying very often at Johnson Hall, came to see Joseph before he sailed. As parting gifts he gave Deseronto and Joseph each a London rifle.

They returned on the ship the *Harriott*. The vessel was at sea for six weeks, taking a southern route in order to avoid Yankee privateers. One sunny morning Joseph and Deseronto were lying on the deck when they heard the lookout shouting to the captain, who also began to shout orders. As they watched, sail after sail was shaken out, and the masts bent under the push of the wind. The captain yelled, "Privateer!" as a hawk-winged vessel with a sharp hull grew large on the horizon. The *Harriott* heeled and righted herself painfully. In the stern two small cannons popped and fell short but solid shot from the raider ripped holes in the *Harriott's* canvas.

Speaking in Mohawk, Joseph and Deseronto agreed to try out their new rifles. The privateer was near enough to bring her crewmen into view. Joseph knelt to rest his rifle on the rail and Deseronto acted as lookout, telling Joseph to aim for the tall captain directing the gunfire. As he came in range Joseph squeezed the trigger and the captain fell from view. Deseronto gave Joseph his gun and said a man in a blue cap was giving orders. Joseph knelt waiting for the *Harriott* to lift on a wave, and with his next shot the blue hat was gone. Deseronto supplied Joseph with loaded rifles and he and Deseronto picked off five men from the raider. Shells from the privateer had shattered the mast and those on the

Harriott were all gashed with splinters and peppered with grape shot. The sailors were screaming, but the captain cursed and bawled at them to climb up and cut away the shattered rigging. Blood ran down Joseph's face and Deseronto was holding his arm. The raider turned away and the *Harriott* limped into New York with ragged sail. To the privateers the incident meant chiefly a regrettable piece of lost booty; to the Mohawks it was a good opportunity to test a hunter's London rifle.

In New York City they met their old teacher, Dr. Wheelock, who asked them to take the American side in the war, or if not, to remain neutral; he asked them to remember what he had tried to teach them. Joseph told him he did recall a prayer that Dr. Wheelock had often used. "You begged we might live like good subjects, to fear God and honour the King." And Joseph added, "This I propose to do."

In New York they also met Lord William Howe, then commander-in-chief of the British forces, who was preparing for battle, and two of his staff: Captain Simcoe, whom they were to meet again in Canada, and Lord Percy, the son of the Duke of Northumberland. A friendship between Joseph and Lord Percy began here that would be lifelong. Brant and Deseronto passed through their loved and abandoned valley in the fall of 1776 and heard on the way that the Mohawks were scattered, some at Niagara and others at Oka. Even Joseph's sister Molly,

Sir William's widow, had been forced to leave because of the threats of the rebel colonial forces, who resented her British allegiance. With her children she was now with some relatives, but Joseph did not try to see her because the rebels were watching for him.

On the way to Niagara he met Kirkland, the Oneidas' missionary, who asked him if he would hold a council meeting with a delegate from the rebels. Since Kirkland had been kind to the Oneidas, Joseph promised, and in the spring sent a message to say he would meet the delegate and Kirkland at Unadilla on the Susquehanna River. The delegate was to be Herkimer, a German farmer, now appointed General in the rebel army. He had been Joseph's neighbour in the valley. Now he was vain about his appointment and, to show off his new power, he took with him to the meeting three hundred and eighty settlers then under his command. The Confederacy did not wish Joseph to meet Herkimer. They knew the latter had no power and it was counted an insult and a breach of etiquette on the part of the rebels to send a delegate of inferior rank.

Joseph had heard rumours that his old enemy Cox of the trading company was on Herkimer's staff, and therefore, as a precaution, he took five hundred warriors with him; these he left behind in the woods and went alone to meet Herkimer, who had drawn a circle on the ground where they were

39

to stand. When they were in the circle, Joseph asked why Herkimer had wanted a meeting and Herkimer replied that he merely wished to talk with his brother, Brant. Joseph was cold. "Do all these soldiers come out of friendship to meet their brother Brant, too?"

Joseph had been right in mistrusting Herkimer's honesty. Herkimer had hidden four settlers (one of them Cox) in the treetops to kill Joseph if he did not succeed in bargaining with him. Joseph, watching closely, saw Herkimer's uneasiness and gave a sudden war-cry that brought all his five hundred warriors around him. He politely thanked Herkimer for the meeting but advised him to go home and stay there.

Kirkland did not appear.

Then Joseph and his warriors went on to Oswego for a war council. All the British officers were there, including Butler from Niagara with his militia. Afterwards the men of the Longhouse held a council of their own and nominated Joseph as their war-leader against the rebels. Sangerachta the Seneca, himself a courageous leader, when Joseph had been appointed to replace him, was the first to say, "I will follow him."

The American rebels had built Fort Stanwix on Indian lands and put Colonel Peter Gansevoort in command over seven hundred and fifty soldiers. The British planned to make their first move an attack on this fort. Colonel John Burgoyne, stationed in Montreal, was the second-in-command of the British armies in America. Lieutenant-Colonel Barry St. Leger, with a mixed force of four hundred British regulars and six hundred "Loyalists" and Canadians, was to march from Oswego and meet General Burgoyne at Albany. With St. Leger was Joseph Brant, leading a thousand Indians.

In August 1777 Colonel St. Leger besieged Fort Stanwix as word came that General Burgoyne had taken Fort Ticonderoga on Lake Champlain. Scouts ran for General Herkimer who lived nearby; he hurriedly called out one thousand of his militia. Most of Herkimer's men were German farmers and frontiersmen who had squatted on the Mohawk lands. They had no battle dress, though a few sported red cockades in their hats. The officers were local gentry in continental blue uniforms. But they were keen for the fight, confident that they could beat the "redcoats" and the "Loyalists", their relatives and former neighbours, who had chosen to be loyal to the King.

Herkimer ordered three scouts to go ahead and enter the fort under cover of night. Three shots by them in the morning would be the signal that Colonel Gansevoort's men were ready to attack the British. Herkimer's rebels would attack at the same time and cut the British down from the rear.

It was a good plan. But in the morning, though

41

no shots came from the fort, Herkimer's unruly men insisted on an attack; he was forced to go with them. It was a breathlessly scorching August day. They scrambled forward in two lines on a forest road which led through a cool swampy ravine. Scouts were not needed to mark their noisy approach. Joseph Brant had laid an ambush in the cool ravine. An American, said to be Cox, Joseph's old enemy, on a white horse led the first of Herkimer's companies. The first shot, which toppled him, was the signal for the wall of dark trees to flame with orange fire from blazing guns.

This battle in the Oriskany Ravine was one of the goriest of the American Revolution. The rebels who had usurped the Mohawks' lands and the Indians who were displaced had such violent hatred for each other that it erupted from both sides like scorching lava. Many fought with bare hands. They battled till late afternoon, and some of Herkimer's advance men fled. Five hundred American rebels were killed and General Herkimer died later. Yet St. Leger did not get into Fort Stanwix and Burgoyne was forced to remain in camp on the Hudson.

The winter at Niagara was bitterly cold in 1777. Gunpowder was scarce, food was hard to find in the deep snows, and many Indians died of cold and sickness. The sight of his starving people filled Joseph Brant's heart with misery as he thought of their lost homes. No help came from Guy Johnson, the

42

nephew of Sir William, who was still Superintendent of Indian Affairs: he spent much of his time in New York City. So Joseph and his warriors decided to make plans of their own for recovering their homelands. If the British did not eventually win these wars the Mohawk lands would be lost forever, but in the meantime some forces must keep striking at the rebels so that precious time would be saved. They could not be homeless much longer; another winter like this would see them all dead.

They knew that the Mohawk country with its fertile fields fed the rebel armies. Quick, hard blows at the settlements would therefore cut off food supplies. So in the next year German Flatts, Andrustown, Springfield and dozens of farms between were hit with these quick, hard blows and were reduced to smoking ruins. Brant's name became a horror throughout the country. The Americans could not imagine that the Indians had any claim to this land and they fought just as savagely to hold it. But Joseph and his warriors took much blame for the violence. The land-thirsty, like the Johnsons and the Butlers and many more, wanted the land which they, too, claimed in the valley, and they joined in the devastation.

George Washington and the American Congress at Philadelphia were besieged with cries for help. They ordered General John Sullivan to advance from Pennsylvania through the Susquehanna valley. General James Clinton was to come from the north and the two forces were to close like a giant pair of scissors, cut off all the Indians and finish them forever. Brant and his small band of warriors tried to divert them with redoubled efforts, but in vain. The armies crawled ahead. Sir John Johnson, son of Sir William Johnson, with about two hundred Rangers, joined Joseph and his six hundred Indians. They made a stand on the Chemung River at Newtown, where they built a long breastwork. But they had few cannon, and their opponent, General Sullivan, had five thousand men well equipped with artillery which soon blasted away the British defences. The rebels were at the door of the Seneca territory and nothing could now stop their entry. The Seneca land was beautiful, but the rebels left great food stocks, homes, and laden orchards all in smoking ruins.

Joseph Brant had failed but he did not stop harrying the settlements for two more years. He could not believe that hard work would not regain the land of his people. Meanwhile, the Mohawks were still homeless.

In 1782 Great Britain made peace with the United States. The Indian lands were made over to the Americans but the People of the Longhouse were not even mentioned in the treaty. Now where would they live? The Indians would have to look out for themselves.

44

In this time of chaos and revolution, personal happiness had come into Joseph Brant's life. He had met Catherine Croghan, daughter of George Croghan, an Irishman. Croghan had been a lifelong friend of Sir William Johnson and he was well known to all the People of the Longhouse. For many years he had been the deputy agent of Sir William in Ohio. The Indians liked Croghan but he too had a full appetite for land and was often enmeshed in mortgages and debts as a result of his land deals. After his first wife died, he married a Mohawk woman with a large land dowry. Their only child was a daughter named Catherine. She had grown into a spirited and beautiful woman, who now became Joseph's wife. More urgently than ever Joseph felt his people's need for permanent homes where they could live as free people in the kindly atmosphere he remembered.

And Joseph saw that they needed new homes at once; he had watched the faces of his people when rumours of the new peace crept in: despondence settled on them like a blight. Major Ross, who had lately been a British officer, had taken part in their last effort in the Mohawk Valley. From his garrison at Carleton Island he reported to General Haldimand, who had succeeded Carleton as Governor-General of Canada: "The preliminary articles of the peace treaty, concealed from the Indians, have now burst out. Will use every means to console the Indi-

45

ans whose resentment grows. Will watch their motions, as I remember what took place at the close of the last war." The "last war" mentioned was the Pontiac war. McLean, another officer, wrote Haldimand from Niagara: "The Indians look upon our conduct as treacherous. The Indians say they were a free people subject to no power on earth. They were allies of the king. He had no right to grant to the United States their rights or property."

The Senecas offered the Mohawks homes on their land at Buffalo Creek. But they wanted to go farther away and to leave soon. A delegation headed by Joseph went to ask General Haldimand where they could have lands. Haldimand offered territory on the Bay of Quinte, which was accepted. Joseph and John Deseronto hurriedly gathered the scattered groups of Mohawks from Lachine and Oka and many other small camps and they began gratefully to build themselves homes again. The Senecas back at Niagara begged them earnestly to settle nearer by, and Joseph went again to General Haldimand. This time it was decided that they might live on the Grand River between Lake Erie and Lake Huron. Joseph also asked that they be indemnified for their war losses as other Loyalists were, so that they could build new homes to shelter them. He received a promise of fifteen hundred pounds New York currency.

Joseph went to the Grand River valley with the Mohawks from Niagara. They were accompanied

46

by some Ranger and Loyalist families. Some of the Mohawks who were already settled on the Bay of Quinte wished to join their families at Grand River, but three hundred of them elected to remain at Quinte with John Deseronto as their chief. They had all been told: "Provisions will be allowed for a reasonable time to the Six Nations in such proportions as the vast consumption occasioned in victualling the Loyalists can admit of." The Indians knew what the "provisions" at Niagara were. What they wanted most was to have their own cornfields once more.

At last they began to settle down. The Cayugas, Onondagas, Tuscaroras and some Senecas had joined the Mohawks. The young men were tireless in their hunting, for good food was the great need. Bark shelters served until a small sawmill provided material for houses—wooden floors and shingle roofs; their fireplaces had chimneys. Soon they were to have a church and a school and they were building a longhouse for a council chamber.

In 1784, Mr. Stuart, who in the old days when the Mohawks were in their homelands had been the minister at Fort Hunter church, crossed the border to Canada. He had been held prisoner for a time by the Americans. A fine reunion took place when he came to Mohawk Village to visit his old Mohawk friends in their Canadian homes. He later wrote of them: "They were comfortably located on a fertile

47

soil. The village had about seven hundred souls."
He was delighted with their beautiful church. "As
they had no stated clergyman at the time, I preached
to a very large audience. It cost me a struggle to
refuse the unanimous and pressing invitations of this
large settlement to remain among them. The pulpit
of the church was trimmed with crimson and the
Creed and the Ten Commandments in the old Mohawk language were on the wall behind it."

Mr. Stuart has also described Joseph as he knew
him: "His influence has been acquired by his un-
common talents and address as a counsellor and
politician by which means he subdued all opposition
and jealousy. His power lay in his strong practical
good sense and ready insight into character."

Now the Six Nations were united in safety but
the long nightmare of uncertainty, cruelty and despondency they had lived with in those past years
would never be forgotten. Joseph, who had seen
Pontiac in Detroit in 1763, had since endured himself
the stresses that had impelled Pontiac's rage to free
the land of alien people. Yet, though he too still
believed that Indian ways and Indian thinking were
good, Brant had seen many new things in his travels
that the Indian children would have to learn from
the white men. With time, he knew, old hates would
die.

He knew that the British needed the People of the
Longhouse, small and weak as they were now, for

Haldimand had said he needed the assurance that the Longhouse stood between him and the tribes beyond the Lakes. When asked, he had kept his promise to give the Indians land for new homes. But they needed more than Haldimand's word to assure them continuing safety. While making their new homes they talked at length about these matters. The Longhouse was broken now because the King had asked their help and they had given it. Now they needed the King's word that he would help them.

The Council settled on a plan. They would draw all the tribes together from the east and the west for a Grand Council, and ask them to cement their bonds in the confederacy pattern of the Six Nations. Then, united, they would appeal to the King. Every move they made was known to the British government. Sir John Johnson in Montreal wrote to General Haldimand in Quebec in August 1783: "Captain Brant, John, Isaac and deputies of the Six Nations accompanied by Colonel John Butler set off for Detroit to meet Cherokees, Creeks and western Indians to strengthen their confederacy by a union of all the nations."

The Grand Council took place at Sandusky on Lake Erie on September 1, 1783. This meeting was not planned by the government, yet John Butler, a Loyalist and a rival of Sir John Johnson in the scramble for a place in the government, had attached himself at the outset. Minor clerks and officials also came from the British headquarters at Detroit and, of course, any kind of Indian gathering always drew traders and rum-selling riff-raff sniffing out business. The British agent from Detroit, McKee, sat himself at the head of the circle as the self-appointed leader. These men were not like Governor Haldimand, who was harsh but honest: they would use any knowledge they could gain of the Indians' plans to ingratiate themselves with higher officials in the British government.

McKee made a speech, addressing the great crowd as "children". There was no response from any of the delegates. Joseph Brant, lame from two old gunshot wounds, rose up slowly. All eyes were turned his way, for to the western tribes he was the link at this council between the two races. He spoke with deliberation, because he knew it had not been planned that these small officials should sit in the council. He called the Indians "brothers and nephews", and told them of their reasons for taking sides in the war. He told them the Six Nations had sent back all prisoners. At the end he said: "Our interests are alike. Nothing should be done unless it was the whole people speaking."

Impressed by this council, Governor Haldimand wrote to the British government in November: "The Indians understand the nature and obligations of treaties as well as the most civilized nations and know that nothing can be binding without their consent. Their general confederacy is to defend their country against invaders."

President Washington took the view that the Six Nations had been deluded by the British. He felt that peace should be made with them on honourable terms, including the restoration of their lands, provided they were amiable. Three commissioners of Congress were appointed to meet them. But Governor Clinton of New York did not agree and he was determined to meet the Six Nations first. He set a day for a general meeting at Fort Stanwix, inventing a pretext to keep the commissioners of Congress away. Delegates of the Six Nations arrived to find Governor Clinton, the New York State commissioners and a crowd of judges, army officers, politicians and traders arrayed to meet them. The Oneidas and Tuscaroras did not come till they were sent for. Their missionary Kirkland sat beside Governor Clinton.

The Governor made a long opening speech addressing the delegates as the "Four Nations" to remind them that the Longhouse Confederacy was broken! At the end he said that New York State, because of suffering caused by the war, expected large cessions of lands and pre-emption rights. The delegates of the Four Nations asked for time for a council and the next day Joseph Brant replied for them. He was as formal as Governor Clinton, saying that the Four Nations had considered all he had

51

said but would first settle with the commissioners of the Congress, for they too had lost much and suffered much. To his anger, Governor Clinton accomplished nothing. The commissioners of Congress were on the way to Fort Stanwix.

Joseph left the young Mohawk Aaron with the other delegates of the Four Nations at Fort Stanwix to meet with them. He himself had to hurry to Quebec because Governor Haldimand was returning to England and he had not yet made out the deed for the lands on the Grand River. Almost his last official act was to sign the deed which read in part: "I do hereby in His Majesty's name, authorize and permit the Mohawk nation and such other of the Six Nations Indians as wish to settle in that quarter to take possession of and settle upon the banks of the Grand River running into Lake Erie." It did not say enough, but it was all Haldimand could say.

The Council had known that the deed would only be the first step; that it would need more than Haldimand's signature to make it valid. The logical move was to send Joseph again to England to get the King's endorsement.

Before Joseph left for England he was informed that Aaron, left in charge of the delegation at Fort Stanwix, was being held prisoner by the commissioners of Congress. He protested in a letter to Colonel Monroe, who had been at Fort Stanwix: "It did alarm me. We had all agreed to restore all prisoners and we have done so." But the news made Joseph so uneasy that he did not leave for England until he was certain that Aaron would be returned.

In England in 1785 he was lonely, and he especially missed Catherine. But he knew she was a tower of strength at Mohawk Village and he drew comfort from the thought that now his people all had homes. He had first to send a letter to Lord Sydney of the Colonial Department and to wait for a reply. The letter asked for the payments for war losses that Haldimand had promised the Six Nations, and for assurance of support in any future war.

Lord Sydney could not commit himself at once but he invited Joseph to Whitehall. Joseph was not unknown there, and he renewed acquaintances. Lord Percy, whom he had not seen since they had met in New York City when the young man was in America with his regiment, was now in England and took Joseph to stay at his home. Joseph let his worries drift away for the time, for Lord Percy was a congenial host and had entrée to all the entertainments. The Baroness of Reidesel wrote of Joseph, "I saw the famous Captain Joseph Brant. His manners are polished and he expressed himself with great fluency." He was again presented at court to King George and Queen Charlotte and the King delighted him with a gift of a fine barrel organ, still preserved in the Chateau de Ramesay Historical Collection in Montreal. He also went on the formal "hunts" at country estates where gun-bearers and beaters did all the work. He said there was a vast difference between hunting for food and hunting for fun.

In April Lord Sydney was ready to answer Joseph. He agreed that the certified losses would be made good. The deed for the lands was not mentioned but Joseph understood that it might need more discussion, and he did not press for it. No definite promises were made in case of another war. Again, Joseph knew the reason, for he had listened to much talk. The business people, the Whigs, were in power in England and they wanted trade in America. Joseph wondered how he could make this plain to the Council at home.

After he returned to Quebec he was uncommunicative when he met the officials and the Lieutenant-Governor of Quebec, Henry Hope, wrote to Lord Sydney saying that Joseph showed a very independent spirit. When he arrived at home in Mohawk Village Joseph found love and peace. The cornfields were beautiful. He also found more of his Loyalist friends, wanting to settle on the Grand River.

The year 1787 is known historically as the Hungry Year. The fields withered; springs and wells went dry; game was hard to find; the people were forced to live on edible roots and fish. Amid these hardships runners brought stories that settlers were crowding the tribes in Pennsylvania and Ohio and the Indians were resisting every inch, though they had little gunpowder.

54

Some of these small tribes, like some of the states of the Union, were trying so hard to make good deals that they forgot the warning Joseph had repeatedly made, that every tribe must deal only through the Grand Council in full attendance. They had tried to deal with settlers on their own terms and had so far barely escaped a war. Then General Arthur St. Clair was ordered by Congress in 1791 to quell all hostilities and finally these tribes faced a real military force.

At the time of the St. Clair invasion in the fall of 1791, Joseph was ill with a heart attack, the inevitable result of his untiring efforts. He sent a strong party of Longhouse warriors under the command of William Johnson, second son of Sir William Johnson, who now lived in Mohawk Village, to join with Little Turtle, a chief of the Miamis, in command of the Indian force. General St. Clair's army, though well equipped with artillery, was almost completely annihilated.

The Congress of the United States was alarmed. They invited a delegation of Senecas to come to Philadelphia to discuss a peace treaty. They also invited Joseph Brant. He took time to analyse what implications his going would have and to discuss it with Catherine, his wife. His people would be pleased; it would be proof that his word was powerful. He was not vain but he had learned that small things were important. Moreover, he thought wryly, it might be advantageous if the officials of the

British government had cause to fear that he might turn to the United States. They did worry. He had many letters from them advising him to refuse the invitation. He decided to go. Catherine agreed with him that it was a good thing to let the officials worry over him.

President Washington welcomed him and made him a generous offer. "I was offered five thousand dollars with my half-pay and pension that I receive from Great Britain doubled, merely on the condition that I work to effect a peace," he later recounted. At the very moment when President Washington was firmly promising that his government did not covet any more Indian territory the American government was expropriating great tracts of land. Joseph knew that by "peace" the President meant that the Indians were to accept whatever border line the United States should set. Washington was surprised when the President's offer was rejected. No one in his senses would refuse such a well-paid commission! The offer was then raised to a gift of land worth a hundred thousand dollars and a salary of fifteen hundred dollars a year. This Joseph called a bribe. Joseph surprised the President still more when he again refused all payments, saying he would in any event do his utmost to have peace. He told his people later: "They might have expected me to act contrary to the honour of the Six Nations and His Majesty's interests."

Joseph found that the President had sent a delegation of Senecas to the west and it was the President's idea of peace to have someone convince the Shawnees and Miamis in the Muskingum country that the United States did not want any land beyond that ceded in the 1789 Treaty of the Muskingum River. The western tribes, unbelieving, were wary, suspicious, and angry. When Joseph reached the Muskingum he was amazed to find that President Washington had sent many others besides the Seneca delegation to make peace for him. One party of envoys had already been taken prisoner. Joseph wrote to the President: "Sending such numbers makes the Indians suspicious of your intentions." In such an atmosphere the parleys could come to nothing.

At home in Upper Canada, changes were taking place. Colonel John Graves Simcoe was named Lieutenant-Governor of Upper Canada, and his residence was established at Fort George. Colonel Simcoe had been a major in the Queen's Rangers in the American Revolution and he had been taken prisoner by General Washington's army in New Jersey. He had also been present at Yorktown when Lord Cornwallis surrendered and he was still angry at all Americans. He and Joseph were on good terms, although Governor Simcoe was firmly opposed to Joseph's plan for the Indian people. The Governor wrote in a report that the independence of the Indians was

Brant's "primary object". He saw it as a part of his own work to defeat this idea and believed the way was to "do it with better presents but let them come by me".

Many letters to and from the administration had to do with the theme, "keep Brant in his place. Do not let him think himself influential." A commission as a colonel was withheld from him for this reason. Joseph knew that the government regarded the Indians as inferior rabble, useful for fighting, bringing in furs or carrying messages, but most of the time merely a nuisance.

He had many worries concerning the Indians in general and concerning himself personally. One special grief had been with him for many years; that was his son Isaac, beloved as his first-born son but unresponsive and difficult to guide. In the time of the American Revolution he had been unable to keep Isaac near him and was often forced to leave him to fend for himself and he thought this was the reason that Isaac grew away from him. He could never win Isaac's confidence, although he never stopped trying. Isaac had gone for a time to school in Philadelphia, and he went with delegations to other tribes many times, sometimes with much credit, for he was fine-looking and could be very agreeable. His father had moments of great pride in him but Isaac brought him his deepest grief.

Isaac lived in his father's house where he was

given every opportunity and shown every courtesy; but he was resentful of his father in every way. He was jealous of his father and his father's prestige, and jealous of Catherine and her children. Drinking rum put Isaac into completely unmanageable moods. Once in a drunken fight he killed a white saddle-maker who was a deserter from General Wayne's American army.

A bitter finish was made finally in a tavern which was also a supply depot. Isaac and some companions were drinking and arguing there and Joseph, who was in an adjoining room transacting business, heard the noise and recognized Isaac's voice. He went in to quiet him, but Isaac in a rage attacked him with a knife and Joseph had to defend himself. In the fight that followed, Isaac was wounded. He refused to have the wound cared for and the infection that set in killed him. Joseph gave himself up and the Canadian court acquitted him. But sorrow almost killed him; he resigned from all his activities and gave himself up to despondency. His People of the Long-house stood beside him in his trouble; they held a council and deliberated on all the facts. Then they sent Joseph a letter, for he had shut himself away from them: "Brother, we have considered your case. We sympathize with you. You are bereaved of a beloved son. But that son raised his hand against the kindest of fathers. His death was caused by his own hand. With one voice we take away all blame from you. We tender you condolence. May the Great Spirit give you consolation and comfort under your affliction." The kindness of the Council was the spur Joseph needed to bring him out of his despair.

The unsigned deed to the Grand River lands had to be kept before the changing governments to remind them of their unfulfilled promise. There was no time for grief. John Norton, the interpreter for the Six Nations Council and Joseph's trusted aide, was sent to England to present to Lord Camden of the State Department the request for the King's signature to the title deed.

A daring new idea was being considered. The Council could sell land to anyone who would pay well and the cash could be deposited with the British government for investment. The interest the money earned would save the people from actual want. When the government officials heard this they flew up like startled ducks. Suppose the land were sold to Americans! Brant would have to be suppressed! Rumours flew around and around like dead leaves. It was said that the Six Nations were going back to the United States, and it was reported "on good authority" that Joseph Brant was dishonest in his transactions. The "authority" was a council of sorts held at Buffalo Creek, now the city of Buffalo, New York. The minutes of the council read: "Brothers, we the Six Nations wish to inform at this time that Joseph Brant has not been conducting himself to the satisfaction of the Six Nations and according to Indian custom he is no longer a chief. All do agree that Joseph Brant is no more to be noticed as a chief." This was signed not by a council but by a collection of petty chiefs, only three of whom were Mohawks. These had come to the council at the bidding of William Claus, the Deputy Superintendent of Indian Affairs in Canada, although there was no justification for his being at any council at Buffalo Creek, in United States territory.

When the Six Nations at Grand River heard of the deposition of Joseph they merely ridiculed the whole affair: "It is not reasonable to suppose we should be dictated to in our business by a council held at such a distance, composed of such members." At this time Joseph was the Superintendent for the Six Nations at Grand River. His own people knew that their Council could be called and presided over only by him and only at Grand River, but William Claus, Deputy Superintendent of Indian Affairs, had taken it upon himself to order their Council to investigate Brant's transactions!

If all this show of authority was for the purpose of intimidating Joseph it failed, for when he heard of the council he merely said he hoped he would find out what he was blamed for. He said he would lay his transactions open before everybody, but a mock council at Buffalo Creek was not the place to do so.

So a true council was called at Grand River and Claus was forced to preside again. He made an opening speech offering condolences to the people for their losses in a recent epidemic. It was coolly received. Then he stated that the reason for the council was to review and question the accounts for cash paid to Joseph Brant. After the statements were read, Joseph Brant laid before the Council an itemized account of all the moneys received and spent on lumber and building materials, on the schoolmaster's salary, on a survey, on medicines, on sending delegates to distant councils, and on buying livestock. The Council, chiefs, warriors and principal women, all unanimously approved the statement. They knew these were Joseph's accounts and were just and true. Led by the chief speaker, all signed the endorsement. They referred to Joseph as their head chief.

At the end, one of the old chiefs reproved Claus, saying, "It was wrong that such a proceeding as the council at Buffalo Creek done by Indians of that territory who had no authority should be countenanced by you." Claus stood rebuked, for he was a British subject.

The real reason for William Claus's enmity appeared later. Joseph knew about the manœuverings that went on behind the scenes in the administration of Indian affairs, the juggling of accounts, and the fight for promotion to ascending rungs of the ladder. Joseph knew men. He knew some of them seemed to acquire and spend much more than their salaries. Whose money was it?

Brant and the Grand River Council perceived that it would be intolerable to Claus if all Indian money did not pass through his hands because he was fraudulently keeping some of it for himself. They saw the irony and the outrage of his report to the British government that he had called a council to investigate the disappearance of the money by having Joseph Brant give an account of the money received for land. The Indians' rejection of his charge against Joseph was never reported. They, the Six Nations, who were now planning another delegation to England to secure a title to their new homes, stood discredited.

In January, 1805, Joseph wrote to his friend Lord Percy, who was now the Duke of Northumberland, telling of Claus and the contrived council at Buffalo Creek and of his deposition as a chief. He discussed the plan for selling enough land to provide an annuity for the tribes and asked the Duke to advise him on the likelihood of obtaining a deed to the land. Later he wrote to the Duke telling of the second council that Superintendent Claus had called for the purpose of bringing discredit on Joseph's administration of Indian affairs, and he expressed alarm about the Governor's attitude: "He will only hear from us through Mr. Claus, the head of the Indian Department, who is our implacable enemy, and from what has passed we are well assured he will do everything in his power to thwart our success."

In his reply in May 1806, the Duke said there was a new administration in the Colonial Department in which William Claus had much less influence. He assured Joseph that the Six Nations should send either a delegation or John Norton, secretary of the Council, or better still, Joseph should come himself and lay their case plainly before the government.

Greatly encouraged, both Joseph and John Norton set out for England. They did not go by way of Quebec, but made their way by canoe and horseback towards New York. But Joseph never reached New York. Another heart attack seized him, and it was with extreme difficulty that he returned home.

He recovered sufficiently to attend a large council at Fort George, near Niagara, in June 1806. The entire Six Nations' Council and many government officials, including Superintendent Claus, were in attendance. The terms of the Haldimand grant were discussed; they were interpreted to mean that any of the Six Nations who chose to settle in the Grand River valley were free to do so, but those who chose to remain in their New York State lands were residents of the United States. Joseph plainly explained his idea of selling some of the Grand River land to provide a trust fund.

Then he spoke directly to Mr. Claus. "It is with

regret we observe you received, as trustee, $38,000 two years ago. You have not since accounted to us for principal and interest or any satisfactory accounting. We, therefore, are so convinced that you have forfeited our confidence that we desire our Great Father will appoint some other person to superintend our affairs." Not mere retaliation—just a simple statement of fact. In due time the "Great Father" appointed a commission and Claus was replaced.

This was Joseph's last council and his last speech. He had a final letter from his friend the Duke of Northumberland, whose early friendship had never wavered. Having been adopted into the Confederacy, the Duke always identified himself with it, for he did not look on his adoption as an empty honour.

The Duke wrote to Joseph, ". . . . There are well-meaning persons here who are desirous of forming a society to better, as they call it, the condition of our nation by converting us from hunters and warriors into husbandmen. Let me strongly recommend to you and to the rest of the chiefs not to listen to such propositions.

"Let our young men never exchange their liberty and manly exercises to become hewers of wood and drawers of water. If they [the well-meaners] will teach our women to spin and weave, this would be of use. . . .

"A thousand warriors, inured to hardship, are a

respectable and independent body. . . . The same number of farmers would hardly rate a small parish, seeking protection from others, scarcely heard from . . . and incapable of defending themselves.

"Some of the persons who propose this plan have their own private reasons. They wish to go over among you . . . to teach you to cultivate the ground. They will show you how a very small part of the land granted you is enough to supply your wants. They will next endeavour to prevail upon you to grant them the remainder in gratitude for the trouble they have had in instructing you in agriculture.

"No, my dear friend and warrior brother, never suffer yourself or your chiefs to be induced by their plausible arguments this way for if you do I foretell you will become a poor, insignificant body instead of a free warlike and independent nation as we now are.

"I wish to see the Christian religion, sobriety and good morals prevail among our nation, but let us continue free, as the air that blows upon us. Let us continue as hunters and warriors capable of enforcing respect and doing ourselves justice. . . . Our pretended friends would soon become our imperious masters."

As far back as 1792, Joseph Brant had received a Loyalist grant of land on Burlington Bay for his own home. It was an average grant, for some men had received larger ones and others somewhat smaller, depending on the number in a family. He had built a neat house which he called Wellington Square.

His family life was divided between this house and the one in the Grand River valley, for the whole family was deeply attached to their home in Mohawk Village, and the councils were always held at Grand River.

Wellington Square was an "open house". Many diaries and letters of that day mention the Brant home and its hospitality. In their early homes, the people of the Six Nations had held many festivals and celebrations. To keep these traditions alive, a May Day gathering was planned each summer, where special honour was paid to the chiefs. Visitors were always welcomed. There was feasting, races and contests, native dances, and, later, Scotch reels. A note tells that at one such festival at Wellington Square in about 1800 more than a thousand people attended. An Irish traveller, Patrick Campbell, left a story of his visit at Brant's Mohawk Village home. Campbell went from Niagara by way of what is now Hamilton. There a man named Beasley kept a trading post and bought furs. Beasley was well known to the Indians; so he accompanied Campbell to the Grand River. On the way, the trader spoke of Joseph Brant: he told Campbell that Joseph was a man of great renown, and that, in fact, letters had recently come from the American Congress inviting him to Philadelphia.

He wrote that they were received most cordially. While tea was being served, Campbell noted the pretty china and the pleasant furnishings of the room. When he met Mrs. Brant, her appearance amazed him. He described her as tall, erect, and slender, with great elegance of looks and deportment. The children were all about, for Joseph was extremely proud of his family. Campbell was astonished at the delicacy of their evening meal, and the later entertainment with music from a hand organ. Joseph, who was just recovering from an illness, went early to rest. As an Irishman, Campbell was particularly struck by the fine bed linen.

On the Sunday they all attended the service in their pretty church, where an Indian lay-reader conducted the services. As Campbell noticed later when he visited the school with its old Yankee schoolmaster and his sixty-six pupils, the standard of reading among them was high. Indeed, Campbell was amazed at the general standard of living, for he visited some homes more comfortable than those that housed some of his own Irish countrymen. And he saw good cattle, also well housed, and much corn stored for the winter. Joseph's people had used their money from land sales for good living.

It has been written that Joseph Brant turned to the church in later life, but in fact his first translation into Mohawk of some parts of the Bible, made when he was a young man, had implanted in him a lifelong interest in religion. As an older man, he worked on translations of the Creed and of some of

68

the key passages in both Old and New Testaments for long hours at a time. To get the full flavour of the words he talked much with those of the older men who spoke the Mohawk language particularly well. They all developed a deep sense of the biblical poetry and style.

Joseph's last months were not unhappy because he was with his people, but he did not think his work was finished. He knew the deepest need of his people was to preserve their identity. Events and actions are not all-important; ideals and intentions are the real forces. The people had always faced facts in the Council where nothing was kept hidden. He could trust to the wisdom of the Council: the people's urge for survival as a nation would come to a full tide in every generation. But he was weary. His last words to John Norton reveal his concern for the future of the Six Nations. "Have pity on my poor Indians. If you have any influence with the great, endeavour to use it for their good." As always, with these words Joseph Brant was trying to bridge the gap not only between Indians and whites, but between the powerful and the powerless, between the rich history of the past and the uncertain future. And it is as a linking figure that we should see him: one of the first Indians to come to terms adequately with the European world as transplanted to America, and yet to maintain his integrity as an Indian. To the Mohawks he was a leader respected and trusted because he lived up to their traditions of social responsibility. The settlers of Upper Canada named a town after this great Indian chief, who might well be taken as a symbol of the maturity of a civilized man.

CROWFOOT

CROWFOOT

THE wide-stretching prairie home of the Blackfoot Confederacy was vaguely known to the world in general as "the wild west" in that year of our Lord, 1821. This old and strong confederation was made up of three main tribes, the Blackfoot, the Bloods and the North and South Piegans. These were all of the same Algonkian strain but spoke different dialects of that tongue. In the Indian way of caring for orphans this Algonkian confederacy had adopted a small tribe from the north, the Sarsi. The Sarsi were of an entirely different stock and spoke an Athabascan dialect but they had shared good and ill with the old Confederacy for long years. The four tribes were completely free to appoint their own chiefs to manage their own affairs and each tribe appointed representatives to the Confederacy Council. It was from these chiefs that a leader for the Confederacy was chosen.

One early historian has written that the Confederates were a proud and pugnacious people. They were certainly a vigorous people who, because they had learned to live in their homeland, loved it and were quick to resent any intrusion, but they were hospitable to many.

The wide prairie land was the habitat of the great buffalo and the people of the Confederacy looked on that animal as their staff of life. Buffalo flesh was their staple food. From the largest hides they made tipi coverings; from the bones and the horns, tools and ornaments; and from the small and softer skins they made their clothing. One of their strong beliefs was that the strength of the buffalo came to them when they ate the flesh and wore the skins. Blackfoot folklore has a legend that runs: "In the beginning a buffalo was placed to hold back the waters. Each year he loses one hair and in every age he will lose one leg. When he is bare of hair and all four legs are gone the waters will rush in again."

Anthony Hendry, a scout and explorer for the Hudson's Bay Company, was one of the earliest travellers to visit the great plains in 1754. He wrote that he was amazed at the great plenty of buffalo. A Catholic priest of the Oblate order named Lacombe, who in 1849 was one of the first Catholics to go to the plains, tells in his memoirs that he had more than once seen an arrow shot by a hunter go clear through a buffalo and fall upright in the prairie sod. "Ah, those were the Indian days!" he wrote.

Buffalo-hunting was a way of life for the Blackfoot people and it was no tame sport. Some of the hunters used lances but the bow and arrow was the favoured weapon. Folklore again has legends of arrows that could magically pass through one buffalo to kill another running beside it. The hunt required courage and community organization of a high order.

In the late summer all the tribes came together for a time of ceremonial dancing and games. When they were about to return to their homes the chief of the Confederacy told his announcer to notify the people that the hunting regulations were in force. This meant that the great yearly hunt was arranged and they must abide by the rule that no buffalo be killed until the chief gave the order. There was severe punishment for anyone who was disobedient and disturbed the herds too soon.

The hunting plan called the "surround" was most used in the period of pedestrian culture when horses and firearms were unknown on the plains. Many small camps were set up as near the buffalo herd as was allowed, for the animals must not be disturbed; if they stampeded they would get out of reach and the hunt would be fruitless. The young chiefs directed the project. They selected the men and the women who crept upwind close to the herds so that the animals would not scent their stealthy approach. The men carried their weapons and the strong buffalo arrows. The women carried the *travois*. A *travois* was an A-shaped contrivance made of two small poles with a platform of laced leather thongs across the widest end. Its first use was for hauling. A dog could be harnessed between the pole shafts, a wide leather band fastened around its shoulders to keep the shafts in place. Freight was tied to the platform. Thus the dogs were great aids in hauling the meat or other burdens back to the home camp. The *travois* was also highly adaptable in the hunt. The young chiefs directed where a row of them should be placed, upright and close enough to be lashed together for a makeshift fence. The women with their dogs crouched behind this *travois* fence while some swift-running men encircled the buffalo herd and drove the animals back toward them. Hunters stationed on both sides of the run began shooting their arrows. As the huge animals raced toward the fence the women shouted and the dogs barked madly so that the buffalo turned again past the hunters who had another chance to shoot them down.

After the kill the chief counted the dead buffalo and divided them equally among the hunters. As soon as the meat was dressed the transporting of it back to the home camps was the next laborious task. The buffalo is a huge animal and no part of the carcass was wasted. A single skin weighs several pounds and the meat from one cow yields about four hundred pounds of food. The dogs hitched to the *travois* did their share but each hunter and each woman was obliged to carry a heavy load.

This pedestrian way of life was changed by the

76

[FACING: *A buffalo hunt*

acquisition of horses. An old tribal story relates that this creature was a gift from the Water Spirit to the Blackfoot people. Of any horse that showed high intelligence or unusual endurance they said that a spirit lived in him.

The ancestry of the western horse can be traced to the Arabian stock brought from Morocco to Spain in the eighth century. When the Spaniard Cortez raided Mexico some of his soldiers were mounted. Later in 1541 another Spaniard, Coronado, an explorer who came as far as Kansas on his quest for cities of fabled wealth in the New World, had many horses with him. But most historians maintain that it was from the later Spanish settlements in the south-western states that the Indian people obtained their horses through trade. These early horses were a sturdy breed. That same visitor, Anthony Hendry, who told of the enormous buffalo herds on the plains wrote also of the horses that he saw in the Black-foot homeland, describing them as "very lively, about fourteen hands high and of many colours". Horses made life on the prairie free and colourful. The carrying of heavy burdens could be shifted to the horse, for a *travois* could easily be built to the size of a horse. For a skilled rider on a well-trained horse buffalo-hunting became a glorious sport and the pride of the Blackfoot increased when horses enabled them to master the buffalo.

Crowfoot began his life when the period of horse

culture was well established on the plains. It was in the year 1821 that a second son came to the lodge of Many Names, head chief of the Moccasins band of the Blackfoot tribe, and a chief of their Confederacy.

It is always a proud time when a son comes to a chief's lodge. The chief feels that he is specially blessed and holds the baby high to the sun to show his gratitude. The mother exults in the knowledge that she has borne a son and will be known as the mother of tribes. The event is celebrated with feasting and gift-giving, drawing all the people together. The gift of "happy children" is to them the greatest that can come to a tribe.

The baby's mother was of the Blood tribe of their own Confederacy. At the time of his birth his parents were in the home camp near Blackfoot Crossing on the Bow River, in territory that is now the province of Alberta. The baby's first months belonged to his mother. She had prepared and decorated the cradle as befitted the son of a chief and she it was who carried it proudly. When she rode her horse she sometimes hung the board to her saddle horn but most of the time the baby saw the world from her back where he was tucked inside her shawl behind her shoulder.

It seemed that as soon as the boy found his feet his father began his training. By the time the little boy was four the back of a horse was as familiar as the

79

ground to him, for with the Blackfoot riding was as normal as breathing. His father put a bow in his hand and he practised shooting it constantly. As he grew older he went on miniature hunts for small game with other boys and with them he learned to herd the horses.

Nemorkan was the first name chosen for this son in his early boyhood, a name which he bore through his training by the wise old chief who supervised the boys. Every means that would produce a hardy, vigorous youth was employed. Diving into icy streams and then racing for two or three hours to a new campsite toughened them for long expeditions. In that day the life of the Blackfoot Confederacy was interwoven with many well-organized military and religious societies. The first of these was a society of two. A young boy would choose another of his age and these two would share their life's experiences. Nemorkan's inseparable companion seemed to be his half-brother, Three Bulls. (This name was common to many Indians on the plains because the buffalo was their symbol of courage. The name Three Bulls implied that the bearer had the bravery and courage of three bulls.) And by this time Nemorkan had another name, a growing-up name. He was Kayastah or "Ghost Bear".

Kayastah had grown and learned his lessons so well that at thirteen his father allowed him to go on his first battle expedition. His older brother, already accomplished in the war games, had won a notable victory when he defeated a great enemy in the Crow nation and for this he was given his warrior's name of Crowfoot.

Some time after this victory Crowfoot was honoured by his father's band. He was sent as one of fourteen ambassadors on a peace mission to the Snake Indians in Montana, a large band belonging to the Shoshoneans. These carriers of good will were waylaid and all slain by an overwhelming force of the very people to whom they were sent to make peace. Angered by the wanton act that had destroyed his eldest son, Chief Many Names assembled the largest war party in Blackfoot history, about ten thousand warriors. He himself was the leader, for he must be the avenger of his eldest son. After twenty days' travelling in the middle of winter they came to the Snake territory. Scouts found the enemy, eight hundred lodges of them, in a strong position. The fight lasted for thirty-six hours, but the fury of the Blackfoot attack was at last victorious. Kayastah, now the chief's eldest son, bore the battle flag in the front ranks and was severely wounded. After the battle his father publicly appointed him his brother's successor in recognition of his bravery. He honoured his son further by giving him his brother's good name. So Kayastah became Crowfoot and this was to be his name for the rest of his life.

Young Crowfoot revelled in these stirring years—years of buffalo hunts and raids for horses and winning honours he could add to his *coup*-stick. The victories in battles, raids or in hunting were called *coups* and each *coup* had a definite value. Every warrior carried a lance or carved stick whose decorations were proof of honours or trophies he had won. It was an honour of the first class to capture an enemy's weapons. (A successful horse raid was an honour of the fourth class.) Some warriors specialized in one kind of *coup* such as killing a buffalo with one shot. The Blackfoot often had small wars with surrounding tribes, the Kootenays, the Flatheads, the Assiniboins, and they fought endlessly with the Crees. They made predatory excursions for horses as far to the south as the Missouri. It was these war games and raids that kept the young men of the tribes alert and enterprising. The older men encouraged these activities, for they kept the Confederacy strong.

Young Crowfoot began to attend and listen in the councils. He became convinced that to speak well for one's people was even better than to be a great warrior, for the Blackfoot were a socially sophisticated people, wealthy in lands, lodges and herds of horses. A tangible sign of their prosperity was the summer encampment where the great circles of lodges could be seen painted with totemic designs of family honours. A good lodge needed twenty buffalo skins for a cover and the many lodges with good new covers were evidence of good hunters on swift horses.

When the time came, young bloods like Crowfoot and his friend Three Bulls bought their memberships in the young men's societies together. These memberships were not inherited or given because of the influence of one's parents but each had to be earned by industry. They were paid for in guns, buffalo skins or horses. The memberships were held by each group for several years, then sold again to the younger men, and others were purchased in the same way. The young men's war societies were responsible for managing the buffalo hunts, policing the camps and scouting in times of battle. The social fraternities arranged contests, games and dances. The most important were the religious societies whose duty it was to regulate religious life. Each group had special costumes and songs and dances to be performed only when the group decided. These various societies were the educational system of the Blackfoot. They were the web that held the people together and they made their life important, gay and good, for each society had special functions answering each need of the community. Wealth could be measured by the number of memberships an individual had held, and leaders of the older and higher societies proudly wore their fine costumes, well trimmed with the white weasel tails which showed their standing.

But rank and wealth gave no title to arrogance, for the best leaders were considered to be those who built a community or band that lived a well-managed life and this concept left no room for mere self-interest. Such leaders in each society held seats in the council of their tribe.

There were numerous society rituals, some highly personal, many connected with the medicine bundles and their variety of articles. These were not objects of worship but symbols. Each society had its own ritual songs that told of the virtue of the articles in its medicine bundle. These bundles were carried for the same reason as amulets or a favourite saint's image are worn by people of other races. The purse-like bag holding the collection was made of fine soft skins with much embroidered symbolical decoration. The bundle of a member of a hunter's society might hold a stone shaped like a tiny buffalo; and a piece of the skin of a rare albino buffalo was always carried because they believed it aided them to a successful hunt. Another article often carried was a curious sample of flint that made fine arrow points. A lock from the mane of a swift and intelligent horse might be carried as a personal fetish. The bundles of the members of the medicine societies held small portions of healing herbs and remedies.

One religious ceremony was the spring celebration when first thunder was heard. This was looked on as a demonstration by the Great Spirit, which they answered by their thanksgiving and an affirmation of their unity with nature.

The sun, too, was highly significant in their lives and customs and had always been venerated by the Blackfoot people. After the winter's bleak cold the people rejoiced when the sun began to warm the earth. Every tipi door faced the rising sun. The seat of honour in the tents was opposite the door opening. The light of the sun was held as sacred, for its warmth was thought to open the eye of the heart so that it could see (or feel) the real meaning of living. This is the reason that patriarchs kept vigil on the hills at sunrise to beg the father sun to shine on his beloved people. The setting sun was ever a reminder of the impermanence of life on earth. But the belief about death was that it was a fitting end to life to sink at the last with the sun behind what they termed the "sand hills", where relatives had gone before.

The Sun Dance was the high event of their ceremonial year. This festival brought the Confederacy together when the saskatoon berries were glowing on the russet-leaved bushes. In its deepest meaning it was a prayer of thanksgiving and a prayer for a powerful new vision or renewal of faith. The medicine bundle of the Sun Dance held articles that were significant to the whole tribe. It held relics of wise old chiefs, mementoes of successful battles and other events as well as the claw of a golden eagle and totemic designs for emblems. For each of these objects there were songs and symbolic dances that told of their magical qualities.

To be performed with adequate reverence and dignity the celebration of the Sun Dance demanded expert guidance. A woman of the Confederacy, someone known to them all for her goodness, after long fasting and prayer would take a vow to assume the responsibility for the preparation and supervision of the Sun Dance. In the time of the berry bush's blossoming in the spring the woman and her husband informed the chief of their band of her vow. He, in turn, sent a messenger with the invitation tobacco and the ceremonial pipe to a brother chief, who would send it on to another, and so on. In this way the message was relayed until all the bands knew of the plans for the Sun Dance. This took many weeks, for the bands might be scattered in their winter camps.

The ritual of the Sun Dance in these days of abundance demanded that there be new lodge covers, and plenty of meat for the feasts—especially buffalo tongues which were their finest delicacy and the only food considered good enough to be used for a thanksgiving. Not any tongues could be used but only the tongues of the bulls, so that their strength would come to the people. Every camp became a hive of activity. The young men organized the hunts, and as fast as the hunters collected the buffalo tongues they were carried to the woman of the vow, who directed her helpers how to dry and prepare them for the ceremonial cutting and serving at the appointed time.

When all was prepared, all the bands moved to the site selected for the Sun Dance. Everyone was dressed in his finest clothing. The men rode their best horses, carrying their weapons and shields; a few carried the sacred drums. The horses had fine new saddle-pads and gaily decorated bridles.

The woman who had made the vow rode a *travois* horse as the leader. Her precious medicine bundle was carried at her back, and on the *travois* were packed the prepared buffalo tongues and other ritual properties. Around her rode her women. Behind were the children. Those too small to ride were carried on the many *travois*, or in cradle-boards on their mothers' saddles. It was a gay yet solemn time of pilgrimage, like other pilgrimages among other peoples.

A medicine man, chosen by the woman in charge and her husband, had the honoured position of Sun Dance leader. Under his direction camp was pitched, with a large branch-enclosed bower in the centre. The centre pole of the bower was hung with offerings. The beating of the drums was soft and gentle and the heads of societies made long prayers. The dancing was quiet and restrained and many of the dancers fasted for the full four days of the Sun Dance.

Self-torture was sometimes practised by the young men who wanted to prove their stamina and to do homage to the sun; but to do so was a matter of choice. Tobacco smoke from the medicine pipes went up to the sun, who would carry the prayers to the Great Spirit. The song cycles were sung fervently, some by the men only and others by the women. Some songs were prayers sung by all the people. The relics of many a wise old leader were held up while songs were sung telling of his days and the good that had come to the people because of his wisdom. At intervals the women who were the helpers cut and served the buffalo tongues and the avowed leader saw that each part of the ritual was rigidly observed.

It was a happy time. Old friends were together. Presents were exchanged and every tipi door was open for visiting and feasting. Before the tribes dispersed for the serious business of the fall buffalo hunt they held games, sham battles and horse races. With the Blackfoot people whose wealth was counted in horses and who were superb riders almost every gathering ended in tests of speed. Every man watched his horse herd all the year for a colt that might show signs of unusual speed, and that one came to be his pride and joy. Horses were not raced till they were at least three years old, for a long course was the rule. Every band of a tribe had its favourite which it secretly trained, and high excitement ended in high stakes, for almost anything but the family tipi might be wagered. These gala days were short-lived.

88

Reluctantly, the camps broke up, for the fall hunts could not be delayed. The long and bitter winters demanded a full supply of food and warm robes and there was great labour involved in their preparation for use.

Spread over the year there had been excursions against old and new foes. These small wars were to remind the Crees and Assiniboins to the north and other tribes to the west and south that encroachments would not be tolerated. There were glories and trophies in all these forays that gave the young men *coups* to boast about and brought stirring memories to the older men.

The women of the plains were the artificers. They worked the hides of the buffalo into velvety softness for baby robes. They made saddles of the tough hides for all the family, child-size to grown-up, with a good surplus for trade. The saddle-pads and other harness for holiday use could be decorated in any fanciful way; even masks were sometimes made for the horses. These women had skilled and capable hands and they brought beauty into tribal life in the designs they applied to the clothing.

These were Crowfoot's people. They were a proud people because they were at home in their own land and equal to its stern demands. The pioneer Oblate missionary said of them in 1865 that they possessed a savage pride, a great eloquence and a love of freedom.

Yet now there was a great fear in them, for the

89

Rider on the Pale Horse ran with the riders of the plains. The new and dreaded disease, smallpox, scorched its way through the tipis of the Confederacy in Crowfoot's sixteenth year. Smallpox was but one of the new sicknesses that came in the vanguard of the newcomers from the east. It was not more deadly to the Indians than the consumption or even the measles that came with it, but it was the quickest of the killers. The sickness itself was loathsome, and to Indians who took joy in a good body the pitted skin, that lasted as long as life if one did recover, was looked on as a blighting reminder. Their medicine men had no remedies for any of the new sicknesses. The tribes in the east had the belief that the traders and the priests carried these diseases in their breath, for the sickness followed their visits.

Four devastating visitations of the smallpox struck the Confederacy in Crowfoot's lifetime and each left many tents of the dead. An old missionary in the west relates that when one of these epidemics was raging in the tipis the chiefs called a council to plan a way to fight this destroyer, and they decided, "This is the white men's disease and he has sent it among us to kill us." The Council agreed that if all the white people were killed the deaths among their own people might stop. They sent out a small war party. Near the home of a missionary, scouts went ahead and were surprised to find him in great sadness because three of his children were dead and others very ill. They had great pity for him but they did not abandon their plan. The party went on to the trading post many miles away. When they reached the post the factor was dead. They reported to the Council that the white men themselves had no medicine for the smallpox.

Crowfoot, Three Bulls and their mother survived these dreadful epidemics, which took more than a fourth of their people. There is no record of these losses but it is said that Many Names, his father, died in the last one. It had seemed that Crowfoot had a charmed life in the battles also, for he took part in nineteen of them. He was wounded six times but the only mark of these wounds was a lameness that remained to the end of his days.

Typical of these small wars was a certain Cree attack in the middle of a wintry night. A small band of Blackfoot had been the first arrivals at the winter campsite selected near Three Pounds, now the city of Lethbridge. Natous, whose name meant The Sun, was the chief of the band and visiting him on this night was Father Lacombe, the priest of the Oblate order who was trying to introduce the Catholic faith to the Blackfoot people. They were all quietly asleep in Natous' tipi when suddenly the Crees attacked, and were overcoming them when Crowfoot with his band, coming into the campsite, counterattacked and drove them off. The Oblate wrote later, "Crowfoot fought like a bear."

Indeed, soon after this he had an encounter with a bear, a grizzly that had caught up a child. Crowfoot, who was mounted nearby, charged with his spear, snatched the little one away, and killed the bear.

When a young man, Crowfoot had married a woman of the same Blood tribe as his mother. Because of his accomplishments and standing he could have chosen whom he liked, but he honoured his mother by having her choose and make the marriage plans. The children of this marriage were sons. Late in his life he adopted a small girl of the Crees because of his loneliness at the death of one of his sons.

In appearance Crowfoot was tall, of slender but sinewy build. He had a fine face with high forehead, good profile and keen, alert eyes. His whole person suggested repose and strength. When he rode his horse in midsummer he held an umbrella over his head. For ordinary occasions he wore deerskin clothing, as did the other men, but for ceremonial wear he had a magnificent robe of buffalo skins worked to a wonderful whiteness and softness, as rich as ermine. It was ornamented with beadwork in a gorgeous pattern. A glowing sun was the central motif on the front, surrounded by totemic designs. A great treasure was his white chimney-pot hat trimmed with a band of eagle feathers. He carried an eagle feather fan on great occasions and at all times he wore handsomely trimmed moccasins. The women of his household had quick and clever hands.

Many of the men were his equals in war deeds and accomplishments for war was a Blackfoot tradition, but long before his father died Crowfoot was the acknowledged young chief, leading the councils by the power of his eloquence. Like all Indians his people had a profound respect for wise speech, and he was proving himself to be one of the nobility, that is, of the orators. Crowfoot had a fine herd of horses and he shared them freely with those in need. The door of his tipi was always open, especially to the young men. As an astute politician, he knew this hospitality added to his prestige. He never abused his power. His father had lived to see him become a chief of his tribe; later he was chosen a chief of the Confederacy.

The traders who came to the plains brought another commodity which could almost be called a suitable companion for the Rider on the Pale Horse. The liquor they carried was as deadly to those who drank it as the epidemics. Some western traders declared they had never sold a single glass of rum to Indians. This could be true. They sold barrels! Many fortunes which later were called respectable began when the traders' craving for money met the Indians' craving for whisky.

But all the Blackfoot did not crave it nor did all Indians. We know that Crowfoot would have noth-

ing to do with it, for, had he done so in this period
when everything Indian was being scrutinized by
alien eyes, such a weakness would have surely been
pointed out in the records of the time. A group of
Crowfoot's own people, returning home after they
met a whisky trader, were refused admission to their
own camp while they were drunk. Making a line on
the ground, Crowfoot defied any of them to cross it
till they came back sober. His brother Three Bulls
more than once directed law enforcement agencies,
after they had been set up, where to find the estab-
lishments of whisky-traders. In one of the Cree raids
on an agency and a settlement at Frog Lake, kegs of
wine from the church were poured out on the ground.

But in spite of all efforts, lawlessness grew. Although Crowfoot made the whisky pedlars unwel-
come and disciplined his own folk, he saw break-
downs in old ways to which he could not shut his
eyes. White people were common now on the plains
and he saw daughters of the tribes taken as wives
by them and later abandoned when these rovers left
the country. The young men often closed their ears
to counsels of the chiefs of their band and in councils were clamorous in their demands to drive all
these aliens out of their lands. They could have
done so easily, for they had plenty of warriors.

The prairies were swept by winds of rumour.
Indians travelled far in their tradings and some from
the east had told the Confederates before that in

lands long their own strangers were crowding in, marking off parts and putting up fences, telling the Indians whose home it was that they could no longer pass over it. These rumours were repeated in the Blackfoot councils and some of the chiefs pointed to the traders who had taken land and built whisky forts. They said, "If we are to have this come to us we will have only the crusts thrown to us. It is better to be killed by bullets than to starve." But in the early 1870's these rumours were not known as facts to the Confederacy, although they were topics of discussion in the councils. The good days of hard riding and bounteous buffalo hunts were still their own. If the young men killed an occasional alien the Council made nothing of it because there always seemed to be more and more foreigners pouring in in the dead man's place.

Indian tribes have frequently been cursed and sometimes blessed by strangers who have come to their homes and taken root there, sometimes for long periods, without apparent reason. Sometimes such visitors have turned out to be fugitives from justice, spurned by their own kind. They were given shelter and hospitality, but later some of them abused this kindness by becoming the Indians' severest critics or even active enemies if that later served their own interests.

The Oblate fathers who had come to the west had stayed in the tipis of the Confederacy but now the

95

Catholic church had opened the first mission. In these years Crowfoot had grown to be friendly with the priests. Father Albert Lacombe had certainly been long enough among the Blackfoot to learn a little of their language and as certainly Crowfoot had learned some of the priest's French, as well as a little English. The road of communication was open to them.

Memoirs of Father Lacombe reveal his liking for the Blackfoot people. He admired their strength and he understood their pride in themselves, their way of life and their love of freedom. They recognized him as a good man for they had good men of their own. But they were not easy subjects for his proselytizing, for their own beliefs were strong. If Father Lacombe frowned on some of them, they in their turn found his ways amusing and laughed at them, calling his crucifix his medicine stick. They compared him to their own medicine men and found little difference. His preaching of punishment after death, however, was a fresh idea. Death, from what the Blackfoot considered natural causes, as in warfare, did not worry them too much. When one of them was dead they said, "He has gone to the sand hills", meaning "beyond the sunset". They killed his best horse to send with him and mourned him as much as they felt he deserved. Their daily life they found very good and for a long time they rejected the idea of misery after death.

96

Another Oblate, Father Constantine Scollen, also spent much time in the tipis. He was described in a diary of the times as "very nice, jolly, agreeable and clever but very homely and weatherbeaten". He was a Dublin Irishman who wrote that he had no desire to return to Ireland but expected to leave his bones in this country.

Jean L'Heureux, who had been born in France, was another guest of the Blackfoot. He was said to be cultured and well educated but he could not speak the English language well nor could he write it. His reason for staying with the Blackfoot was never very clear, but he later called himself an interpreter. At some time he had studied for the priesthood. Occasionally he posed as a priest and he even performed marriages.

Two other men, James Bird and Jerry Potts, were early plains residents. Both were sons of Hudson's Bay men who had married Indian wives. James Bird remained with the Indians, working for the Company as an interpreter. Jerry Potts was hired by the Royal North West Mounted Police as a guide when that force came to the west in 1874, and he remained with them for many years.

These early arrivals in the Blackfoot country were presently followed by hordes of adventurers. The market for buffalo skins had been steady, for they were always in demand for warm robes and coats, but soon industrialists in the eastern cities found the

97

tough hides made long-wearing machinery belts. There was suddenly an insatiable demand for skins and buffalo-killing became an industry. Killers came from afar to share in the profits.

Gold was discovered across the border in the state of Montana, and this brought a wild rush of thousands of prospectors to burrow in Indian lands. Many tribes were uprooted from the land they called their own. As one history book delicately states, "It caused an unrest among them." It also caused many of them to flee into Canada for refuge and for food.

As early as 1830 the American Fur Company had established a distillery at the mouth of the Yellowstone River, using the corn grown by the women of the Gros Ventre tribes. The principal article for barter at the trading posts was this cheap whisky and lawlessness on the plains swelled and festered.

The United States then revived an old law forbidding the sale of whisky or other intoxicants to Indians. This law was not valid in Canada, where new trading posts sprang up that were supplied from American bases. These posts, soon called whisky forts, had to be loop-holed for defence and one of them had an ambitious cannon mounted on its roof. This arming was necessary, for the forts were often raided by rival dealers or too-enthusiastic customers. The wary trader operated through a wicket in the door and through this opening the customer thrust

98

the robe or bundle of skins for which he was paid
two cupfuls of the liquor from the tub at the trader's
elbow. A quart was the price of a pony. The most
infamous of these places was called Fort Whoop-up
and it was right in the Blackfoot country. There was
great misery in the tipis, for the women of the bands
were the real victims. The men sometimes fought
each other in drunken frenzies, and for the protection
of the children and of the men themselves the women
took all the guns and knives into hiding with them
until the men had regained their minds.

The North West Mounted Police rode in in the
heyday of these entrepreneurs and scattered them
like the chaff they were. This force, organized to
bring law and order to the plains, came on the scene
in December 1874. They were only three hundred
men spread out in several depots and they had a
grim struggle for years, for whisky vendors did not
easily give up their good trade; when they were suppressed in one place they rose up in another and they
sometimes carried on trade from a moving wagon.

The chiefs of the Confederacy welcomed the band
of red-coated men with their good guns, which gave
the laws teeth to grip and hold the outlaws and took
them out of their country. Fort Macleod, built for
them near the international border, had a stout little
jail from which the traders found it impossible to
bribe their way out. Fort Macleod was named for
James Farquhar Macleod who had come to Canada

from the Highlands of Scotland. He had long been a professional soldier and eventually became a commissioner of the Mounted Police.

Colonel Macleod went with Crowfoot to meet the other chiefs of the Confederacy in whose territory he was. He later wrote that he was "received with stately ceremony", and found the chiefs "intelligent men who conducted the interviews as dignified gentlemen". The chiefs told Colonel Macleod they were grateful to the Mounted Police for getting the wild traders with their arsenals and bad whisky, both of which killed their young men, out of their land. Colonel Macleod cultivated the friendship of the chiefs for a reason. He had a mission which he intimated first to the Council when he told them that great men of the country were to come for they wanted to make a treaty with them. The word "treaty" had no meaning to them.

Crowfoot's liking and friendship for the Oblates grew, and Father Lacombe spent much time in Crowfoot's home. Crowfoot's friendship for these men from the east grew to include Commissioner Macleod.

The Hudson's Bay Company, which had held sway over the wide western lands for decades, had always discouraged settlement. They knew it would be the end of the fur business with the Indians, on which the prosperity of the company was built. However, when the new government of Canada finally persuaded this powerful company to sell its exclusive trading privileges for a million and a half dollars, immigration began to grow in earnest.

The men of the church and the law who were cultivating the friendship of Crowfoot and his people knew of the impending changes. In 1870 the plan for the transcontinental railway was the talk of the east. It is a possibility that they may have told Crowfoot of what was to happen, but all that the general body of the Confederacy saw was that more and more settlers were all about them; and that made them restless.

The local traders warned them that the buffalo would disappear. One of their own old prophets, Many Stars, had long been shouting, "Have your good time now. Buffalo will soon leave. They will be shown to you only by the white men. There will be no hearthstones to mark where you have camped! You will make a living from the earth, sell grass, sell rocks. The only skins will be your moccasins."

The Confederacy watched Crowfoot, but he was not bothered by such talk. He was learning from the white men ideas that seemed strange to his people. The young men looked askance at a ruling he made after a successful horse raid on the Crees. It was understood by everyone that horses taken in a raid were likely to be stolen back. That was an old rule. It was not possessing the horses so much as the danger of taking them that made the game exciting. Such raiding was not directed toward conquest of enemy territory or extermination of a tribe. Creeping into a guarded camp and coming away with the chosen horses without blood being shed was a *coup* to gloat over at society gatherings. Yet they all knew it was a recognized act of aggression. If some were killed on either side—well, one must die sometime!

When Crowfoot ordered that the horses taken from the Crees by his own band, the Moccasins, were to be returned to their owners, he was obeyed. He could not give this order to other bands for he did not have the right, but he advised other chiefs to do it also. Some even took his advice, for they respected him, but now they did not understand him. He had gone ahead of them. Crowfoot was pioneering in social relationships, for Father Lacombe had discussed with him the brotherhood of all men beyond one's own people.

The international line between Canada and the United States had little meaning to the Indians of the plains. They had followed the vast buffalo herd to the south and back to the north as the seasons came; that was their way of life. All the tribes knew the limits of their territory and guarded it. They had special places for the home camps where there was good grass for the horses as well as wood and water for the people. All these places were well marked and well beloved, for the bones of their grandfathers were there.

The tribes over the border lived in the same way. More and more settlers wanting lands were pressing them from all sides. The gold finds, as in Montana, brought hordes of outlaws and ruffians running over the country like rats. Treaties made by the United States government with the various Indian tribes were violated as soon as made. If the Indians began reprisals over outrages, soldiers came and forts were erected. It was a time of misery.

In December 1876, fresh from one of these disasters, Sitting Bull with some thousands of his Sioux people and many horses crossed the border from the south and made camp near Wood Mountain. He told the North West Mounted Police who went to find the reason for the intrusion, that he and his people were driven out of their country and they were only looking for peace for they had not slept sound for years. They only wanted a place where they could lie down and feel safe. Because Queen Victoria was its ruler the Sioux called Canada "the grandmother's land".

Crowfoot and his people were in camp in the Cypress Hills, east of Medicine Hat, and Sitting Bull went there to pay a visit. Crowfoot made him welcome in his tipi, for they were old friends, and he made a feast in his guest's honour. Sitting Bull had long admired Crowfoot's wisdom and his good government of the Confederacy. He said he would like Crowfoot to give his (Sitting Bull's) young son his own name. "We will be friends to the end of our days. My children will be your children and yours will be mine." He gave Crowfoot many horses as gifts.

Major Irvine of the police described Sitting Bull at that time as "Rather short of stature with a pleasant face. A mouth showing great determination and a fine high forehead. His frequent smile brightened his face wonderfully. His personal group of warriors, about forty-five of them, were very tall and muscular." Sitting Bull was amazed when he learned that if a white man shot an Indian the "Red Coats" would hang the white man! And he was more astounded when he found that Crowfoot's people actually turned over their Indian lawbreakers to the Red Coats for trial and they were not shot!

From Canada, Sitting Bull led reprisals on the American settlers in his own part of the country but Crowfoot and his people took no part when their help was asked. His young men were not mercenaries fighting for pay nor did they join war parties purely for love of fighting.

The Canadian government was in a quandary. The United States government sent delegates of American officers to the Sioux, promising them farms and rations if they would return. Sitting Bull replied, "I will not be a reservation Indian." When the clergy were included in the delegation the Sioux were always kind to them for they had no war with the missionaries, but the army officers were scorned.

Yet there was no land for a home in Canada for Sioux Indians. Canada would not force them to leave. They were self-supporting for they lived on the buffalo, but they could not be permitted to stay indefinitely. While a second deputation from the United States were in their camp, a long line of Nez Percé people, wounded and bleeding warriors and women and children, dragged themselves wearily into the circle of tipis. These were victims of skirmishes between the Indians and the United States army, and their coming ended the conference. The Sioux could have attacked the army officers then but they let them go quietly.

The heralded proposal from the "great men" in the Canadian government was that the Blackfoot Confederacy cede to the government their ancient territory for Canadian settlers. The Indians met the representatives of the government at the Milk River in southern Alberta to discuss this proposal. A story remembered from that time tells of the man who spread a sheaf of dollar bills on the ground, and said, "This is what the white man trades with. This is his buffalo robe. As you trade with skins we trade with these pieces of paper." Crowfoot took up a handful of clay and dropped it on the fire and cooked it. Then he said to the visitor, "Now, put your money on the fire. See if it will last as long as the clay." The man replied, "No, my money will burn because it is made of paper." Crowfoot said, "Your money is not as good as our land. The wind will blow it away. The fire will burn it. Water will rot it. Nothing will destroy our land."

They were told that the treaty would ask that they make their marks on a paper that said "No more wars with the Crees." Would the Crees know this also? They knew that many settlers would come but the land still had many buffalo and there would be enough for all. That was what made it the good land the settlers wanted to share. And the marks on the paper would also mean there would be presents and money and that more money would come each year.

But no longer were the councils peaceful. Pride of ownership was strong in the Blackfoot people but the things they felt they owned were tangibles, like many horses around the camps of strong, well-covered tipis and memberships in the societies with the finest clothing. A treaty that would take away their home-land was beyond their imagining, since to them their wide land was as the air one breathed. The chiefs looked to Crowfoot for guidance for he knew more of the ways of white men, but they could see he was profoundly worried. There was a new austerity in his manner. The picture of the Sioux and Nez Percé refugees was fresh in his mind and it made his heart sick. The Oblates had let him know the truth: a treaty would mean that there would be soldiers to enforce it.

A trader, son of an Indian mother and a white man, warned, "All you Indians, all the chiefs have not tried to send these mounties back east. They are going to give pieces of blue-backed paper. That is a dollar but it means there will be no more buffalo." But this was a story they could laugh at, for every tribe had piles of buffalo skins for the trading.

The unrest in the councils spread through the camps and when the too-eager Oblates went to the old good chief, Natous, urging him to use his power to have Crowfoot make a good decision, Natous sent them away abruptly, saying, "When the time comes Crowfoot will speak." The Blackfoot would have to live under white laws. The priests said there would be no other way. Would these new laws, unknown to all of them, let them preserve the way of life that had built the people and made them respected on the plains? This was the worry that gnawed Crowfoot's mind. Father Lacombe busied himself by calling on all the chiefs of the Confederacy and some of them were offended by this. They were suspicious, for they had decoyed the buffalo into traps themselves and the eager priests now seemed to be trying to lure them into a snare.

On September 18, 1877 the "great men" came. The Honourable David Laird, Lieutenant-Governor of the North West Territories and Indian Superintendent, was one of them. He was a Canadian from Prince Edward Island. The other was Commissioner

James Macleod of the North West Mounted Police. The Blackfoot had come to trust him when they saw that the Red Coats under his command gave him the same loyalty Crowfoot had earned from his people. In Scotland the forbears of Commissioner Macleod had known plenty of conflict, when border wars raged between England and Scotland and many of the settlers on the Red River in Manitoba were crofters or small farmers who had been dispossessed by tyrannous landlords in Scotland. Commissioner Macleod had sympathy for the Blackfoot, but he also had a stern duty before him. With the Honourable David Laird he was to lead the Blackfoot to "cede, release, surrender and yield up" to the government of Canada fifty thousand square miles of their prairie kingdom. For this land and in "extinguishment of all past claims" each man, woman and child was to be paid at once twelve dollars. Later there would be other benefits like cattle, medals, implements and a yearly payment forever of a few more dollars for each member of the tribe, with the chiefs in power getting the most.

The meeting place for the council was at Blackfoot Crossing, a favourite home camp of the people and a place of unusual beauty. On this September day the river glimmered in the sunshine and the cottonwoods and willows shone with golden leaves. The coulees were all aglow with the bronze and russet browns of the wild rose and buffalo berry bushes. The Confederacy made camp, a settlement of a

thousand lodges. The Indians were in their finest
clothing and each cooking fire sent a smoke signal
high in the clear sky. A large tent had been erected
to serve for a council chamber at one end of the
encampment. The bell-shaped tents of the Mounted
Police shone white at the other. The commissioners
arrived in great style, escorted by officers of the
police in their red coats and spiked helmets. After
all were assembled in the large tent the council was
opened with a fanfare from the police band.

Neither Crowfoot nor his brother Three Bulls
would accept any small gifts from the commissioners
until the people had heard the terms of the treaty
read. James Bird, the son of a Hudson's Bay Company employee who had taken an Indian wife, was
the interpreter for them. They were very quiet and
they asked time for conferring. They still had no
real knowledge of the small acreage that ceding
would confine them to, but the Confederacy trusted
Crowfoot completely. If they had not, a rebellion
might have flared up, and this could have had dis-
astrous results. Crowfoot was under tremendous
pressure.

He went to stay alone in his tipi and the commissioners waited impatiently. At last he gave the word
that he would sign on the morning of the fifth day,
September 22nd. Having made the decision, overwhelmed with worry and sorrow, he moved his tipi
out of the camp circle to a lonely place.

When the morning of the fifth day came a cannon

was fired from the hill as a signal that the council was to begin. The cannon boomed again as Crowfoot made his mark on the long parchment of the treaty, the bagpipes wailed gaily and the Union Jack was hoisted. The other chiefs of the Confederacy made their marks, Three Bulls signing for the Blackfoot.

The Honourable Mr. Laird led off the speeches. He loved to make speeches. He spoke easily and cultivated an elegant manner. He also spoke intimately of the Great Spirit who had made them all brothers, the white man and the red, saying, "We should take each other by the hand," and "the Queen is pleased that you have taken the Mounted Police by the hand and helped her by obeying her laws. If this is done they will always be your friends and on your side."

When Crowfoot made his speech he turned to Governor Laird, giving him a feather he had drawn from his eagle's wing fan, saying, "Keep us like this feather forever." He expressed his worry and foreboding in this allegorical way. In time the young men, deprived of their life of hard riding and responsibility for providing the food for their people from the hunts, would be like the pliable feather he held. When that time came he hoped the commissioners would have patience. He felt that it would take a long, long time for his people to accept a changed way of life that would make them into another people. A little later when the medals were presented to the chiefs some refused them. They knew themselves to be chiefs, their people knew they were chiefs. They needed no medals, and did not wish to be under any obligation to the commissioners.

By way of entertainment, after the signing was completed, the Confederacy staged a sham battle such as they enacted after a Sun Dance ceremony. This was really a mounted war dance. Hundreds of gaily dressed warriors encircled the whole encampment, performing riding feats and firing guns into the air. It was so realistic that the officials were alarmed and the warriors enjoyed their uneasiness. If the Red Coats could parade their strength, the Confederacy could put on a good show too.

The prospect of the Indians' having money for spending had brought scores of traders with goods, and business was brisk. There would be many new blankets for the cold winter ahead.

The commissioners went their way and they were well pleased. They felt they had subdued the wild people of the plains. The Confederacy encampment broke up to hurry their arrangements for the fall buffalo hunt. Surveyors immediately were busy marking off the new lands.

The busy life of the people flowed on.

In 1878 at the time appointed for the first treaty payment, the Indians were shocked when they received less than had been agreed upon, and Colonel Macleod had no good explanation to give them. Some of the Indians met the situation by using another of their names and collecting twice, but this was frowned on by the chiefs. The promised cattle had not come either.

After two years Sitting Bull was still in Canada. The government of the United States could not coax nor yet force him back. And it was apparent that as long as the herds of buffalo were the food supply of the Indians they could not be subdued or controlled as the American authorities saw fit. So it was decided that the buffalo must be destroyed. The great buffalo herd had long been divided by settlements across its migratory paths from the winter feeding grounds in the south to the summer pastures in the north. The eastern market for buffalo hides had sent hordes of buffalo-hunters to the west and the southern herds had been wiped out by relentless killing. The American government saw this as a step towards controlling and settling the west, and approved the wholesale slaughter. After the skins were taken the carcasses were left to rot on the plains by the thousands. But the vast northern herd still remained, and the American hunters could not follow them into Canada. The year following the treaty the buffalo hunts still supplied the Blackfoot with all their needs.

American troops had tirelessly patrolled the border, on watch for Sitting Bull and his Sioux. When the herds came down from Canadian pastures the troops were ordered to prevent the buffalo returning to Canada. A gigantic round-up and slaughter was carried out by the hundreds of skilled hunters and skinners assembled for the purpose. To be sure that no small herds strayed off and escaped killing, the Canadian pastures were fired. Sitting Bull and his Sioux must be brought to their knees.

Edgar Dewdney, an Englishman, Indian Agent in the North West Territories, reported to his superintendent, "in 1879 a series of prairie fires were set at different points simultaneously as if by prearrangement. The country north of the border was burned over from Wood Mountain on the east to the Rockies in the west and almost as far north as Qu'Appelle." A note in the report of the Hudson's Bay commissioners stated, "The general impression is the fires were started by the Americans to keep the buffalo south of our border." When Lord Lorne, the Governor-General of Canada in this period, sent a confidential protest to the American State Department, it was passed over unnoticed. These vast operations were carried through without news of them getting back to the east until they were over. With irony unhappily typical of their history, the Indians of the plains have been blamed for the sudden total extinction of the northern buffalo herd by their improvidence and wanton wastefulness.

Though the trickery behind the extermination of the buffalo could be concealed, the effects could not.

The Indians of the plains were immediately rendered utterly destitute. Never before had large numbers of them, whole communities, known hunger from actual scarcity of food. Now they could not find enough meat for the children, for even the small game like deer had been destroyed by the fires. They were reduced to eating gophers and other rodents, and in desperation a few even ate horsemeat. Some of the old people starved to death. Then in the midst of the desolation, the herds of horses suffered an epidemic of mange.

The Canadian government had decided that the Confederacy could hunt as usual, but with a gradual drawing-in of the police rein they would be made to stay on the land reserved to them. Over a period of years they would be given the promised cattle and implements. Then, very easily, they would all become farmers.

The government received a rude jolt when in the summer of 1879 forlorn lines of hungry Blackfoot people came to Calgary and Fort Macleod. They shot cattle at sight and ate them, cattle intended for the rations of the police at Fort Macleod. When they were at Calgary the men went to Inspector Denny of the police and demanded food. He gave them what he could for he was afraid to refuse, and sent in haste for Commissioner Macleod to know what could be done for these starving people. Commissioner Macleod did not desert the Indians in this extremity, but met them at Blackfoot Crossing, the place of the treaty. When Crowfoot and Natous asked for the cattle pledged in the treaty, Commissioner Macleod had to tell them it was not part of the plan that these cattle be used for food. They were to be used to stock farms.

Food had to be grown for the police, and there was a farm station at Pincher Creek. Commissioner Macleod sent a quick call there for a man who could teach the Indians gardening and the care of cattle. This would take time; so he issued rations to tide them over, but this supply could only be temporary. The government's leisurely plan for settling the Confederacy on farms would no longer serve. It had to be done immediately!

Happily, it was treaty-money time and, best of all, the report came that some buffalo had been sighted toward the east. The Confederacy people used their treaty money to buy a supply of food and set off to hunt. It was arranged to leave the weak and old behind because it would have been impossible for them to keep up with the hunt. It was a great relief to the Commissioner to see the hunting parties go. It gave time for the government's plan to be set in motion.

The Blackfoot hunters went as far south as the Yellowstone, where food was plentiful for a time. Away from the laws of the new Canadian treaty the young men could fight back if they were attacked.

Coups could be counted and the Sun Dance lodge set up in gratitude. They visited their relatives, people of their Confederacy in Montana. Life was normal and good again. But the next spring no buffalo could be found. The horses and hides the Blackfoot could spare for trading for food were soon used up. The chiefs faced the fact that a return to their own land was inevitable.

From the time they reached the treaty site they began a new way of life. The farm teacher from Pincher Creek had built a house to live in and there were a few huts the old people had made. There was a small herd of cattle and land had been broken for root crops. The government's plan had begun to operate. These people, who had long been the only planners of their lives, were bending to an unknown yoke that would often chafe. Their opinions were not asked, nor were their views on methods and values consulted. Ordered about like children or morons, their only defence was apathy.

The new food was distasteful to them. Whereas the old buffalo diet had made them a strong, hardy people, the fat pork or bacon of inferior quality from Ontario farms was horrible to them, for no one knew how to cook it. No one had an appetite for the potatoes and turnips from the farm manager's plot. The tipis all had many sick and dying people.

As hunters, the men and women too had worked hard for their required food, shelter and clothing.

Their ritual life was forever bound up with their daily life. Belonging to a society was proof of worth, worth earned by daily conduct. Their beliefs and superstitions had grown out of their tradition and experiences and they clung to them tenaciously. They valued the knowledge of the song cycles that belonged to each society. They valued the ability to conduct a rite with dignity. These were intangibles but they were the web of the realities of life.

Crowfoot had never been a gardener, and the other chiefs also were against this new way of life. He continued to tend his herd of horses and they increased. The Blackfoot could not forsake Indian ways so quickly. At this time Crowfoot, having devoted the sixty years of his whole life to achieving Blackfoot ideals, was honoured by his people for his wisdom and goodness. The other chiefs acknowledged him chief of chiefs. So even now, though he had signed the white man's treaty, there was no rebellion against him, for he had earned their trust.

The men of the Confederacy felt at such a disadvantage now that they were sullen and despairing. Their old, good way of life, they could see, would have to be discarded like old tipi covers. The new had already begun, with regimentation and petty restrictions they resented bitterly. Their old associations with traders and settlers had been of their making. They had goods to trade. The deal was made and the trader left. There was self-respect in this. Now the farm manager began to tell them what they could sell or he would sell for them. The hardest thing of all to bear was the contempt. Church and state combined in their belittling attitudes, often unconscious, to everything Indian. To promote the work of salvation it somehow seemed necessary to represent the Indians as godless and murderous. Yet the irresponsible and cynical murderousness of the whisky-trader went unchecked.

Crowfoot gave no sign that he blamed the officials or pitied the people. The Confederacy, plunged in this whirlpool, must find a way out or die.

Sitting Bull and his Sioux were still in Canada, "the grandmother's country". The slaughter of the buffalo had brought them to the brink of starvation, as it was intended to do. Pressure was increasing in Canada for their removal. A report of the Mounted Police at that time stated, "The very name of Sioux strikes terror into the hearts of the settlers." Yet they were law-abiding and had done no harm to anyone. In 1868 Sitting Bull with about twelve hundred of his people went to Fort Qu'Appelle and asked Superintendent Samuel Steel of the Mounted Police, who was in charge there, for permanent territory in Canada. Mr. Steel sent the request on to Agent-Superintendent Dewdney. Mr. Dewdney came to the fort and told Sitting Bull there was no land for them in Canada for they belonged to the United States. But he was kind and suggested that he supply them with rations till they crossed the border. Sitting Bull recognized the inevitable and the offer was taken. The Sioux folded their tipis and left for their old homes.

In 1883 the Canadian Pacific Railway, in process of building, came into the Blackfoot country. Crowfoot was ill with a throat ailment and his people were worried. The railway had begun to lay tracks on Confederacy lands without asking permission. Crowfoot objected, "This is no part of the treaty." His people moved tipis to the land and camped there, saying "No" to the surveyors. Commissioner Macleod was sent for, but they held their ground. The Commissioner sent telegrams to the government at Ottawa and a compromise was made. "If the railway is allowed through your land up the Cluny Hill to Gleichen we will give in return the same amount of land on the south side of the river as we take." The Blackfoot Council saw this was fair and the railway went forward. Because of this fair dealing, Indians never hampered the Canadian Pacific in its operations. As a representative of the Confederacy, Crowfoot was given another medal by the railway company, good for transportation over their line.

A new kind of war, a religious struggle, came to the Confederacy. The busy and manœuvring Father Lacombe was continually among them, but they could see no reason why he should take any part in their councils and they resisted his influence. Presently the Catholics demanded of the government of Canada that the administration of these Indians be under the control of the Roman Catholic church. Then the Protestants from the east raised their voices in dispute, for, as they pointed out, they had sent missionaries also. Their missionary reports said in effect, "The Blackfoot Confederacy was less amenable to Christian influence than the wood or mountain tribes. The great freedom these people have known made the restraints of Christianity hard for them to accept and needed stern measures, even starvation, to enforce."

In 1884 the Catholic church finished and made ready to open the St. Joseph Industrial School near Calgary. Father Lacombe was searching the different bands for children he felt could be moulded to Roman Catholic doctrines. There was much bitter Indian prejudice against white ways. The men who talked to them of the new life were pushing and overbearing, and they lacked the dignity and courtesy of the Indian leaders. Also they were the bearers of the new diseases that had taken Indian people by the hundreds. The older people said the children should not have the new schooling, for they had been a strong, happy people before. Very few young parents were willing to have their children leave them to go away to the new school. Those who let theirs go soon went for them, for the tipis were too lonely without them and the children were lonely at the school. Father Lacombe implored the government to starve these people into submission, and he asked the Mounted Police to bring back by force the children who ran away.

All these conflicts swirled about Crowfoot. He cushioned the blows as well as he could for the people, but there was little he could do.

Another plains people, the Métis, were also suffering from the destruction of the buffalo herds. The Métis were the descendants of French adventurers, voyageurs and other early travellers who had married "daughters of the land" or Indian wives. Of these the largest number had lived for years as a group in the Red River country in Manitoba.

When Canada purchased territorial sovereignty from the Hudson's Bay Company, the Métis and other settlers there, to their consternation, were not notified of the purchase. Surveyors suddenly appeared on their land. Led by one of their own men, Louis Riel, the Métis either rose in rebellion or, discouraged by this callous treatment, moved farther north and made new homes in Saskatchewan north of the wide area burned to kill off the buffalo herds. Buffalo supplied their needs while they were attempting to establish new homes and start farming. The anticipation of a northern railway had brought settlers into these new settlements also. The Red River pattern of events was repeated, but in this case the Métis had no other place to go. Appeals to the government brought no response.

When the Confederacy was in Montana on the

last hunt, Crowfoot had met Louis Riel who was teaching in a school there. (Riel had been well educated in Montreal when a boy.) Crowfoot and Riel had discussed the Métis and the Cree people who were neighbours and sympathetic to the Métis. Crowfoot told him the Confederacy had now a treaty of peace with the Crees, their one-time foes. In the talk of rebellion and war, Crowfoot made it clear to Louis Riel that the Blackfoot Confederacy would take no part. "We are at peace," he said. The Métis implored Riel to return to Saskatchewan to lead them in their second rebellion, but the Confederacy refused to join them, even though the young men would have welcomed the excitement of a battle, bottled up as they were on their reserve territory.

At least one white man thought this might be an opportunity to divide and rule the Indians. Sir John A. Macdonald, Prime Minister of Canada, in a letter of March 1885, to Lieutenant-Governor Dewdney, suggested using the Confederacy against the Métis and their Cree allies. "It would not do to encourage an Indian war," he wrote, "but I understand the Crees dread the Blackfoot like the devil. Now, a corps of scouts under Crowfoot might be formed and kept west but the information should be widely spread among the Crees and half-breeds that a Blackfoot force had been prepared. This might have the effect of producing a panic among the Indians." Sir John did not consider that Crowfoot was long past his warrior days. It seemed such a good idea to him that he could not wait for Mr. Dewdney's reply but wired, "Do you approve enlisting a small body under Crowfoot?" Mr. Dewdney was not very interested in the Métis. He replied cautiously, "Think it might be of great service if we could secure the assistance of a few Blackfoot as scouts. It would keep the balance quiet while they were at work." Then he did nothing about it. It seemed he hoped that Macdonald's mind would be distracted to other matters, for in that day of distances the Métis of Saskatchewan were far away from the politics of Ottawa unless someone powerful thrust them to the fore.

Dumont, a Métis leader with Riel, who had failed to get help from the Confederacy, said in a speech, "You would not know the Canadian Indian. He is all changed. Pride, vigour and sturdy independence all gone. The loss of the buffalo made the change. His living is gone. His very life is gone. He does not like the rotten pork the government gives him. He is sick. Smallpox and other white men's diseases kill them in hundreds. He talks of uprisings but he does not have it in him any more. He is just full of grievances. The only difference between the Métis and the Indians is that the Indians have a treaty."

When Crowfoot had met him in Montana he had told Riel that his people would not go to war and Riel made no offers to them when he returned to

123

Canada to lead the Métis in the Saskatchewan Rebellion of 1885. But Poundmaker, a chief of the Crees, allies of the Métis, sent a courier to Crowfoot. They were holding a quiet council in Crowfoot's home but somehow news of this emissary's coming to the Blackfoot had been sent to the Mounted Police and they made one of the few breaches of the courtesy that had marked all their dealings with the Indians by invading the privacy of Crowfoot's home and arresting Poundmaker's Cree courier. Crowfoot's bitter resentment of this was outspoken, but speech was his only available form of protest. Otherwise the rebellion passed the Blackfoot by, except that they took in some of the refugees; a group of Cree women and children fled to them and were cared for.

But only in small ways could Crowfoot now protect his people. For instance, the fat pork so objected to made them ill in the hot weather. (The blue ink stamp of the packer also amused them wryly: they had seen the tattooed arms of a policeman, and had noted the resemblance.) Crowfoot took the matter of the bad meat seriously and went to Magnus Begg, the agent, who agreed the pork would not be issued again till cold weather.

The councils had lost their authority, for the chiefs were not asked to share in new responsibilities. All they were asked for was obedience, like small boys. It was a belittling and bitter experience that could have quickly flashed into revolt.

Attempts were made to reconcile the Indian to the lot imposed on him, attempts that were often well meant but usually inadequate because they were confused, ignorant and fundamentally lacking in respect.

The Canadian government and the Canadian Pacific Railway invited Crowfoot and his brother Three Bulls, North Axe of the Piegans and Red Crow of the Bloods to go on a trip to the east. This trip was to be a "lesson in civilization" for them. Later some of the Cree chiefs were added to the group. But when the time came, Crowfoot's beloved son had just died. He was in great mourning, even ill. By the custom of his people he could not take part in any public affair before the funeral rites and the period of mourning were over. He had many other troubles, for recent deaths in his family had greatly impoverished him; yet reluctantly he agreed to go.

Father Lacombe and Jean L'Heureux both greatly desired to be the official guide of the party. The first telegram from the government designated Father Lacombe, who was most anxious to be seen in the east with the famous chief of the Blackfoot, but Jean L'Heureux hustled off with Crowfoot and Three Bulls and had travelled some distance when, after more telegrams, Father Lacombe with the assistance of Hayter Reid, an agent, had them held until the whole party was assembled and they could leave with some dignity. They were finally divided into groups,

Father Lacombe with Crowfoot and his brother, Mr. L'Heureux with the men of the Bloods and the Piegans, and the Cree chiefs with their own agent, Mr. McDonald. They went as far east as Montreal, where the Canadian Pacific Railway was their host. They were well entertained and given more medals. When they came back to Ottawa, the government and that city honoured them. The Mayor made a flowery speech, attempting geniality by the use of a few eastern Indian terms like "manitou" and "wampum" which had no meaning to plains Indians.

But by this time Crowfoot was really very ill and sad and had no heart for festivities, so that he went directly home from Ottawa. The rest of the party completed the tour of Ontario to their great enjoyment. Mr. L'Heureux's expense account was questioned in Parliament later. In defending it he revealed that he had been the victim of some Indian humour. He wrote that he thought it much better to spend money for a few cigars than for a small steamboat or half the Ottawa museum which the Indians as a joke had asked him to buy for them; at Winnipeg they urged him to purchase a monkey and a machine to make thunder!

Crowfoot never again fully recovered his health. The lingering character of his illness would indicate that it was tuberculosis, or consumption as it was called then. His people cared for him like a beloved father, and he talked much to them of the new life they must follow. He begged them to cultivate the friendship of good people as far as they were able.

But for all his bravery in attempting to meet new conditions and adapt to a new way of life, for all his intelligence and sensitivity to the drift of the times and the circumstances, it could not be concealed from his people that a great chief, a great hunter, brave warrior, eloquent spokesman, intelligent diplomat, good man—was hunter, warrior, effective spokesman no longer. In his approaching death the decline and death of the old Indian ways were all too intimately represented. All his wisdom, all his strength and gentleness, all his peace-loving efforts to solve their problems had not established the old Confederacy in the new confederation called Canada. Not with anything like the old dignity. Not like themselves.

In the fall of 1889 he told them he would die in the spring. In April he sent for Father Doucett of the Catholic mission and Agent Wheatley, saying he wanted to make his will. His horse herds had increased and he directed that these be divided among his relatives. To his wife he gave one of his medals, his house and other property. The rest of the medals he gave to his brother, Three Bulls. Gifts from the tour he gave to Mr. L'Heureux and to the medicine men around he gave fifteen horses.

Two days before he died he sank into a coma.

Even the medicine men thought it was death, but they waited and in the evening he revived. He took a small portion of food and enjoyed a pipe. All his relatives had gathered about and he asked them not to mourn for him. On Friday afternoon when he died his people obeyed his wish. But according to their custom, his favourite horse was shot for his use in "the land of the sand hills beyond the sunset".

In his last hours he said, "What is life? It is the flash of a firefly in the night. It is the breath of a buffalo in the wintertime. It is the little shadow which runs across the grass and loses itself in the sunset."

So passed one of the good people who have walked the earth.

ORONHYATEKHA

PETER MARTIN

ORONHYATEKHA
Peter Martin

EVERY family has in its history one member who
sets new standards and blazes new trails, even
a family where great achievements are usual.
Such a member was born in 1841 to the Martin
family of the Mohawk tribe in the lands of the Six
Nations. The records of his career are sparse, for
Peter Martin was a man who claimed little for himself, and made his mark in actions rather than in
written documents. Nor did anyone in his own day
or since think his story sufficiently dramatic to merit
a biography. Yet, though his life is not part of the
official history of Canada, his influence was far-
reaching—into the lives of hundreds of thousands
of Canadians of all races.

The Six Nations had been dwellers in the Grand
River valley in Ontario, then called Canada West or
Upper Canada, for fifty-eight years. They came as
pioneers after the American Revolution, for they had
held sacred an ancient treaty of alliance with the
British made by their "grandfathers", as they termed

their ancestors; their first settlement was known as Loyal Village, and later, Mohawk Village. As the families grew they spread along the river banks, and the family of George Martin grew to be the Martin Settlement, a little community which came to be known for its musical people.

In Upper Canada by this year 1841 there had begun the stirrings of nationhood, for the union of Upper and Lower Canada had just taken place. Toronto, the capital of Upper Canada, had grown to be a city. But at Loyal Village, when Peter Martin was born, Mohawk tradition and Mohawk ways were still strong and vigorous. Historians of that period like to picture these Indian folk as Stone-Age primitives but the Six Nations, particularly the Mohawks (for they dwelt in the east) had lived in neighbourly fashion for more than half a century with the Dutch and later the English settlers in their New York State homeland before their ancient confederacy had been ripped apart by the fury of the American Revolution. Many of their old white neighbours had come with them to Canada and settled around them in their new land and there was little difference between the Canadian homes of the two races.

Still the Six Nations clung to the old ways that seemed good to them. The Indian speech was well known and well spoken but almost all the young people were bilingual, speaking and writing both

132

Mohawk and English. No child in that time was allowed to grow up without a formal Indian name. The name chosen for small Peter Martin was Oronhyatekha, which, when translated into English, meant "Burning Cloud". There must have been a touch of prophecy in this chosen name, especially in the word "burning", for that best describes the energy and zest that marked Peter Martin's whole life.

The George Martin family was a large one of sons and daughters and Peter was one of the younger members. He first went to the small school near his home; with this he was soon finished, but good fortune opened the way for him to attend the Wesleyan Academy at Wilbraham in the state of Massachusetts. This was a small but good school founded in 1817. Only by great effort could Peter Martin afford to stay there. To earn his living he turned his hand to any chores that came his way. Later in his life he told with pride of the enormous pile of wood he had cut for forty cents, saying, "It kept me in bread even if I had no butter." In his outreach for learning his family helped as they could.

Even at that early age Peter Martin presented a good appearance. Indian women were ever accustomed to fashioning clothing and his older sisters made him fine-looking suits of English cloth as well as the white shirts he liked and wore all his life. In his final year at the Academy he took the highest standing in his class. This success, he would laughingly explain, was owing to the fact that he was always grateful to sit down for rest and study after he had finished the chores which paid his way.

While he was away in Massachusetts, a school was opened just east of the Martin Settlement and on his return he was hired for a year's teaching. This provided the funds so that he could again go off to school, and this time he chose Kenyon College at Gambier, Ohio. Kenyon, an Episcopal school for men, was within his means so long as he accepted a few additional duties. Even so, he took the first two years in one and finished Kenyon in three years. By this time Peter Martin knew what he wanted to do with his life, for he had set his heart on becoming a doctor of medicine trained in a Canadian university; he returned to Canada and studied one year at the University of Toronto.

The Prince of Wales, later to be King Edward VII, came to visit Canada in 1860 and great receptions were prepared for him all across the land. The Indians of the Six Nations planned to present the young prince with their own address of welcome and their gifts. Because of his accomplishments and his experience in meeting many people, Oronhyatekha was chosen by the chiefs to present their welcome to His Royal Highness. And this historic event again opened the door of opportunity to Peter Martin.

In this his twentieth year Oronhyatekha had reached his full height of slightly more than six feet.

134

[FACING: *Oronhyatekha, wearing full Indian dress, welcomed the future king of England.*

He was slender with an erect and powerful physique. His brilliant dark eyes were alert and often shone with gaiety, for he had a naturally happy manner. He was always perfectly groomed so that his whole presence was one of great dignity.

For this splendid occasion when he would address the future king of England, his Council wished him to represent them wearing full Indian dress. Again the work of his devoted sisters produced a fine costume ornamented with their handsome beadwork. The young Prince Edward at the time of his first visit to Canada was the same age as Oronhyatekha. He, too, was slender and erect, in every way the fairy-tale prince. The Prince and his party were impressed by the fine reading of the Six Nations' welcome and the Council was deeply proud that they had a speaker who could carry their tradition of eloquence into the English tongue. The later inquiries the Prince made interested him still more and he asked the Council for the full story of Oronhyatekha's struggle for an education. The remarkable report of it led the Prince to invite the young speaker to go to England for further study, and being practical, not merely impulsive, about the matter, he put Oronhyatekha under the direct care and influence of Dr. Henry Acland.

Dr. Acland, later made a baronet for his life's work, was Regius Professor or King's Physician at Oxford University. All the honours conferred on him were well earned, for he was always a student. Two of his keenest interests, art and archaeology, were so ardently pursued by him that they became important subjects at his beloved university. But whatever concerned the welfare of his country claimed his first attention. His searching studies and his writings on public health undoubtedly influenced Peter in directing the latter's attention to the social responsibilities of his profession.

So it was in these happy circumstances that Peter Martin went to England and spent three good years at Oxford. With stimulating associates, his acute mind expanded and grew and he upheld there his fine record as a student. The kindness and friendship experienced at this time set the pattern for his later life. But he also was practical, for he never lost sight of his goal, to be a physician in Canada. At the end of three years he returned to his native land. Dr. Acland always spoke of him with great affection, saying, "No son could be dearer." This friendship never wavered. Later in Dr. Acland's life, as he watched the development of his old student, he said of Oronhyatekha, "He is a rare fellow man!"

Soon after his return from England, Oronhyatekha married Ellen Hill of the Mohawk community at Deseronto. She was a descendant of John Deseronto, who with his cousin Joseph Brant had held the Six Nations together through the bitter years after the American Revolution.

In the long-delayed land settlement after the American Revolution, the first home offered the Six Nations was on the Bay of Quinte, or "Kenty" as some old maps designate it. Governor Haldimand, who was then the king's representative in Canada, said he felt safe only when he had a shield of Six Nations warriors between him and the wild west. But the Senecas, the western confederate brothers who were trying to remain in their ancient lands in western New York, protested that this new settlement of the Mohawks was too far from them, and that they needed them nearer. Again lands were asked for that would be large enough to provide homes for all of the Six Nations in addition to the Mohawks. When finally the land in the valley of the Grand River was settled on, three hundred of the Mohawks elected to remain on the Bay of Quinte with John Deseronto as their chief. The rest of the Mohawks and their brother tribes, with Joseph Brant as chief, founded Loyal Village on the Grand River. But through the years a close relationship was maintained with the Mohawks of Quinte. And so it was natural that the daughter of Deseronto should marry Joseph, the second son of Joseph Brant. A granddaughter of this marriage was Ellen Hill, Oronhyatekha's Ellen Hill.

She was a high-spirited, gifted and adaptable young woman, and the marriage was a happy one. Their home was always a centre of activity and kept

138

pace with the achievements of the master of it. Visitors to the Martin home wrote that Mrs. Martin was "unwearied in her attention to the comfort of her guests and there always seemed to be room for one more".

After his marriage in 1864, Oronhyatekha had still to finish his final college year at the University of Toronto and get his medical degree. These were the stirring years when Canada was growing into a nation. Politics was the great and continuing occupation. Everyone was in a ferment over the confederation of the provinces that was soon to come. Also, the abortive and ridiculous Fenian raids from across the border made all Canada conscious of the possibility of a war with the United States. It was inevitable that so vigorous a young man as Oronhyatekha should become a private in the University Corps of the Queen's Own Rifles; this interest in the militia held him for many years.

Quickly after his graduation, the new Dr. Peter Oronhyatekha Martin and his capable Ellen set up a home and a practice at Frankford, a village near Belleville and Deseronto. The willingness for public service that marked his whole life began to be apparent here and the young doctor was soon elected the first secretary of the Hastings County Medical Association, which he had helped to organize. After some years in Frankford the Martin family decided to move when an opportunity for advancement came

139

in an offer of a partnership with Dr. Lucas of Stratford. Even while they were building up, as they soon did, a flourishing practice in Stratford, Dr. Martin was also an officer in the 28th Battalion. His energy seemed unlimited. A brief fling in politics at this time was another interlude for the Doctor. He took charge of the canvass of the township of Wallace on behalf of the Conservatives. So well and vigorously was this campaign managed that a feared defeat became a victory. Out of this grew a warm and lasting friendship with the Conservative leader, Sir John A. Macdonald. Later Sir John recommended an appointment for Oronhyatekha as Government Consulting Physician to the Mohawks at Deseronto, and the Martin family left Stratford for Napanee.

Life at Napanee was a pleasant interval. Mrs. Martin loved being near her people and she persuaded Dr. Martin to establish the country home at Deseronto which later meant so much in their lives.

Yet the yearly salary of five hundred dollars as the government doctor at Deseronto was inadequate, especially as the family was increasing in its numbers and in its needs. Now there were a daughter and two sons. So Peter made a brief attempt to be a merchant: he bought a half-interest in a general store at nearby Mill Point. The enterprise convinced the Doctor that his wife was right. He was no merchant! The partnership in fact went into bankruptcy largely because of the Doctor's kind heart, for he could not refuse credit to anyone. After some litigation he took over a debt of about two thousand dollars and to pay it he gave a mortgage on all his property, including his horse and buggy! It was absolutely necessary to consider a new practice somewhere. Two possible openings, one at Buffalo, New York, and one at London in western Ontario, were available. He chose London, and the family was happy in the Canadian decision. They left Napanee in 1873.

For the next half-decade the Doctor devoted all his energies to his profession. He was a good doctor, for his natural courtesy and happy, sympathetic heart coupled with his exceptional training, education and ambitious energy could only have a good result. He became well known as a diagnostician— again keeping to a fine old tradition. In the early days of the Indian folk the men who were responsible for seeking and finding remedies for their ills from the roots, barks, and herbs of the land were tireless in their searching. It has been said by present-day researchers, Dr. Charles Banting for one, that these ancient medicine men had done the "pharmaceutical spadework in North America".

Dr. Oronhyatekha was holding to yet another tradition of his people. In the old days the whole life of the Six Nations and many other tribes was interlaced by societies, from the blood-brother society

141

and the "Three Sisters" service groups for the youthful members to the Matrons' Society and the councils of the sachems. Researchers tell us that these were examples of fine creative social planning for they met normal needs at all age levels.

Dr. Oronhyatekha often laughingly confessed that he was a "joiner". The urge to identify himself with the life around him was always very strong. While still in school he had joined the Good Templars and at times he had assisted in organizing more temperance groups. Later in his life at the world gathering of Templars in Edinburgh he was elected Grand Templar, head of the International Good Templars of the World. He never lost his interest in military affairs and was always an ardent rifleman. He was on the first Canadian team to go to the Wimbledon "shoots" (later the Bisley Competition) with Colonel Skinner in 1871. These Wimbledon competitions were established in England by the National Rifle Association and their purpose was to "encourage formation of rifle corps and the promotion of rifle shooting as a national pastime so as to make the rifle what the bow and arrow was in the days of the Plantagenets, the familiar weapon of those who stand forth in the defence of their country". At this first "shoot" the Doctor became internationally known for his skill as a rifleman.

At that time, when differences of religion were of exaggerated importance in Canada, the Protestant

Orange Order was strong in Ontario and Dr. Martin became an ardent Orangeman. When the Grand Orange Lodge convened in Belfast the Doctor was in the Canadian delegation to Ireland. Yet he had many cherished and lifelong friends in Catholic French Canada with whom he never lost touch. At the same time he was also a Scottish Rite Mason and for some time he was the editor of their publication, the *Masonic Tablet*. He liked and respected the kind of men he met in these societies and they in turn valued him for his ability and integrity.

The Martin family found living in London most agreeable. School life for the children and church life for the family brought many interests and they participated in all the church and community activities. The Doctor's good work gained a welcome for him with the members of his profession. His patients liked him for his skill and, when they came to know him better, for his big heart, for he had a rare quality of sympathetic understanding and he never forgot a kindness. Few men have had so varied a collection of people they called friends, and he was never too busy to give aid where he saw the need. And soon he saw a new and systematic way of taking care of many family needs into which his medical practice gave him insight.

In England's early days the forests and woodlands were the properties of the reigning kings, who employed many men in their protection and care.

These men were called stewards, woodwards, and foresters, according to the duties they performed. Their shelters in the forests were called lodges. In 1745, at Knaresborough, Yorkshire, these men who worked with the trees formed themselves into a guild or union as workers in many of the other crafts had done, taking the name the Royal Order of Foresters. They also developed a system of mutual assistance and a secret ritual. The groups about the land were called lodges or courts and their meeting places became known as lodge-rooms. In time the name was changed to the Ancient Order of Foresters and members bound themselves together in a co-operative scheme for life insurance. This society had been introduced into North America at Brooklyn, New York, in 1864 and in the following ten years it grew to include sixty-four lodges in several states and Canada.

As the membership of the order grew in North America the American lodges, embarrassed by the slowness of the heads of the order in England in the settlement of their insurance claims, made the hard decision to break their ties with the English order. After this the American lodges called themselves the Independent Order of Foresters. They also had a plan for mutual insurance and fraternal organization.

The first Canadian lodges were organized in Ontario at London. In the report of the Most Worthy High Chief Ranger, Robert M. Cordes, of Cleveland, Ohio, the head of the American courts at that time, there appeared this note: "During my visit to Canada in February last to the courts of London, Ontario, I (upon solicitation of nearly every member of the Order) issued a special dispensation to Court Dufferin, No. 7, London, to allow the said court to initiate one Doctor Oronhyatekha, a gentleman of Indian parentage who was highly recommended by everyone who knew him."

At that time the Constitution and Laws of the order read that the membership was limited to "white males of twenty-one years or over". The special dispensation was passed granting the Court Dufferin their request to admit to their membership Dr. Peter Martin.

Later an echo of this discriminatory clause was heard in a court of law at Chatham, Ontario. It happened in this way. A lodge under the auspices of the Independent Order of Foresters had been organized at Chatham. After the installation a large section of the members decided to hold to the English parent lodge, the Ancient Order of Foresters, rather than to the newer American Independent Order. In leaving, the secessionists removed with them all the properties of the Independent Order, so that this group was forced to bring suit to recover their regalia and moneys.

Because he had been by this time elected Chief Ranger of the Ontario courts or lodges it was Peter

145

Martin's rather unpleasant duty to represent them at the trial at Chatham. The secessionists, holding to the English name, asked that the case be dismissed since the representative of the new Independent Order was not a qualified member because of the race restriction in the constitution. The counsel for the seceding group read the clause in the Constitution and Laws which limited the members of the orders to "white males", and he pointed out that since the Doctor was an Indian he had no legal right to be in the courtroom to represent the Independent Order of Foresters or any other order. Dr. Oronhyatekha had never felt his race to be any hindrance. He was proud of his fine old family and prouder still of his Indian birthright. In fact, he was an authority on their history. He was also, fortunately, a master of debate. He sent the whole courtroom into gales of laughter when with a disarming smile he said to the opposing counsel, "You see you do not understand the Constitution of the Order. What you have quoted was only intended to exclude those who belonged to a race which was considered to be inferior to the white race. You will find the Most Worshipful High Court of the Independent Order of Foresters legalized my admission because they acknowledge the fact that I belonged to a race which was superior to the white race and, therefore, not under the ban of the laws of the Order." The lawyer, redfaced, began to apologize. He tried to assure the Doctor, as the

146

court officers repeatedly called "Order, order" to the uproarious courtroom, that he had no intention of casting any reflection on his race. But Peter Martin had won the day by his charm, courage and good humour. Superior races? Inferior races? Nonsense. Eventually the discriminatory clauses were dropped from the Constitution.

Dr. Oronhyatekha grew to believe in the insurance plan of the Foresters as a thoroughly democratic idea. It could be developed into a protective scheme every family could afford. In the next months he travelled six thousand miles at his own expense organizing new lodges.

Because of divisions in the ranks, some lodges deciding to hold to the English, some to the American order, reorganization became necessary. A convention held for this purpose at Ottawa in 1881 elected Oronhyatekha, M.D., the Supreme Chief Ranger. This was a doubtful honour. The national order found itself with a loyal remnant of three hundred and sixty-nine members and a debt of four thousand dollars.

On the other side of the ledger was a new interest in the Order of Forestry in the other provinces. With zeal inspired by their leader the continuing members revised and greatly improved the by-laws and ritual and organized many new lodges. From this time Oronhyatekha, M.D., devoted his life to fraternal insurance. And it was not only the insurance side

of it that interested him. As a doctor he saw the
therapeutic value of fraternal visiting of the sick, for
already he was aware of the psychological aspects
of illness. In one way and another, "beyond all
question he planned, acted, and lived for that great
order".

At the High Court session of the Ontario lodges
in Toronto in 1883 a presentation was made to Dr.
Oronhyatekha. "The gratitude of the entire membership for your never-tiring zeal and energy in
advancing the interests of our beloved order is yours.
It has quadrupled the membership roll and you have
never considered yourself or the interests of those
dear and dependent on you in your work for us. We
can never repay you for your efforts in placing our
order in so prosperous a condition. To mark our
gratitude we ask you to accept this gold watch."
Inscribed with the engraved crest of the order, the
watch was the Doctor's lifetime treasure. In his
reply to the convention he said it marked the friendship, the sincerity and integrity of the men who
worked with him, men prominent in the church, the
law, education and the business of Canada who
were first of all humanitarians.

Dr. Oronhyatekha's appointment forced him to a
decision he found most difficult. He loved and enjoyed the work of his profession but the demands of
his office as High Chief Ranger for Ontario took him
away more and more from his medical practice. The

148

need to move the executive headquarters of the order to the capital of the province settled the matter.

The Martin family moved to Toronto but the regret they felt at leaving London was alleviated, especially for Mrs. Martin, by the prospect of living nearer their own people. It had been decided that the Deseronto lands were to be the home for all of them. Both the Doctor and Mrs. Martin loved the Mohawk speech and at the Pines, their home near Deseronto, it was always spoken. The Doctor, who was famed for his command of the English speech, often said the Mohawk tongue was a language of witticisms. At this time an English periodical wrote of him as being "calm, courteous and imperturbable. He is a master of debate, as smooth and incisive as a scimitar. His quickness in breaking an argument of his opponent is extraordinary, admirable, and always kind." Unfortunately, we have been left almost no written examples of his speeches.

Dr. Oronhyatekha in his forty-first year was tall and arrow-straight as in his youth, but inclined to the portliness which was a characteristic of the Martin family. He was always elegant and faultessly groomed. People sought him, for his friendliness was unbounded. His conversation is said to have sparkled with his knowledge of men and books. In a social gathering of congenial friends it was his delight to start the group singing. His strong baritone voice never tired and in his enthusiasm he would catch up a plate or a book and tap on it like a tom-tom to carry the beat.

In his many trips about the world he had been an ardent collector and his museum was his retreat. The whole family loved beautiful china and the family home had treasured pieces by famous makers which were enjoyed in daily use. His wide-ranging interest had built up collections from many countries. And he particularly liked articles that people had used in their daily lives. He had some pestles an Indian medicine man had used in his preparation of remedies and a collection of presentation medals and gorgets. His love of arms was shown by his sets of old guns and powder horns, and all types of bows and arrows.

The Doctor refused all suggestions that he participate in politics for, after his brief early flurry in Wallace Township while at Stratford, he had decided that party politics had no place in his life. But he was untiring in his study of fraternal organizations. He served as the first president of the Canadian Fraternal Association and later became the head of the international organization. With his board of management he worked out revisions and improvements that made the Independent Order of Foresters a leader of fraternal orders all over the world.

This steady growth made larger accommodations necessary. In Toronto the cornerstone of the long-planned new headquarters was laid by Lord Aberdeen, then Governor-General of Canada. Lord Aberdeen was himself a Forester, and his presence made it a full-dress occasion with parades and fanfares. This edifice, known later as the Temple Building, became a landmark in the city. In its day it was known and described as "the finest office building in Canada".

The phenomenal growth of the order was justification of the years of arduous work, of study and planning. A sound financial system was built up with the cost of management kept at a minimum. This was always the firm policy.

Dr. Oronhyatekha had long held the belief that a truly fraternal brotherhood should consider the family as a unit. If the head of a family passed away leaving minor dependents, the Doctor felt convinced that those so left should be looked after by the order until they were able to care for themselves. This ideal resulted in the creation of the Orphans' Fund, thus making the children of deceased members wards of the order. There was also provision for sanatorium care for members contracting tuberculosis. "In the hearts of orphans snatched from poverty and of once strong men provided for in their helplessness there will ever be thanksgiving that he lived," someone wrote in an article eulogizing the Doctor's plan. Incidentally, this work emphasized the link between Oronhyatekha's medical and fraternal interests.

Hard work he always welcomed, and he had carried a double load of leadership during the twenty years since he had been made the head of the Good Templars of the World. He declined to be a candidate again. Their official paper, *The International Good Templar*, reported: "Dr. Oronhyatekha rounded up his career as manager and commander-in-chief by presiding in such a way that he captured everyone present. His administration has been wonderfully successful. He leaves the chair with a large balance in the treasury and an increase in membership as well as a better feeling on the part of the members than we have ever known. Our membership, the wide world round, not only admire his splendid abilities but they love him as few men have ever been loved in our society."

A list of the names of the men associated with the Doctor on the various management boards of organizations of all kinds is like an index of a work on the builders of America. He always pointed out that it was because of such men that the Order of Foresters, in particular, had reached its high place. It was his firm belief that because he had been a member of a large family he worked best with a group. The Doctor always kept a watchful eye on his family, for the Martins had branched out in many directions, even to the stage. Any one of the clan struggling for an education or in other need could count on a timely lift from him.

152

In the early summer of 1881, catastrophe struck the people of the London vicinity, the Martins not excepted. Besides their daughter, Garaquena, affectionately pet-named Bena, they had two boys. So much had Dr. Oronhyatekha wished to keep strong his ties with his beloved English tutor, Dr. Henry Acland, that he had divided Dr. Acland's name between the boys, Henry and Acland.

Springbank Park was the favoured picnic land of the whole of the London area. It could be reached by train or boat and either way the trip made a pleasant little excursion. The stern-wheeled, two-decker steamer which made the run was called the *Victoria*.

May 24, the traditional picnic day, was chosen by one of the churches for its annual outing and the whole Martin family looked forward to the day they had planned to spend together. At the last moment an emergency prevented the Doctor's going but he insisted that Mrs. Martin and the three children go on the train with their friends as they had agreed. At the end of the day the party decided to return by the boat. In the late afternoon on the return to London the little steamer *Victoria* was too heavily loaded with tired picnickers, and as she laboured along she simply collapsed and fell apart, throwing the six hundred passengers into the Thames River. Many were crushed by the falling timbers of the steamer; it was always considered miraculous that more were

153

not lost. Henry Oronhyatekha, the young son of Dr. and Mrs. Martin, became separated from his family party and was drowned.

Henry's parents took him home to lie in the churchyard at Deseronto. Mrs. Martin never fully recovered from the worry and the regret that the decision to return by the boat had been hers. The country home, the Pines, at Deseronto became dearer to her, and the family spent as much time there as the Doctor could spare. He was deeply interested in farm stock and farm management. In time he had quite an extensive farming operation which was cared for by his brother Simeon, a veteran of the American Civil War. When Mrs. Martin was there no one in the community faced a weekend with a scanty supply of food, for the old and the ill were never neglected. On a Saturday morning it was her great pleasure to fill her little buggy with baskets of supplies which she delivered to them herself, without a trace of patronage. She was "a woman of rare strength and beauty of character, with a remarkable graciousness and strength of character".

When the twenty-first anniversary of the Independent Order of Foresters was to be observed, it was decided to mark the occasion by a weekend celebration at this Deseronto home of the Martins. No lovelier spot could have been chosen to entertain such an international gathering. The guests included Colonel A. B. Caldwell, the founder of Forestry in America, and many more executive officials. Excursion boats brought hundreds more and it was a gala time with a special service of thanksgiving at the historic church on the reservation.

The executives of the order, in gratitude to Mrs. Martin for her hospitality and knowing her love for beautiful china, gave her a magnificent dinner service. To the Doctor they presented an illuminated address bearing the signatures of his colleagues. The Doctor replied for his wife and for himself, ending his short and moving speech in this way: "Sometimes too much is made of men who simply do their duty."

The Doctor had been anxiously watching the health of Mrs. Martin, for ever since the grievous experience in the disaster of the *Victoria* it had steadily declined. She died in March of 1901.

Dr. Oronhyatekha was now sixty years old. In spite of his private grief, his professional eye was as bright and humorous as it had always been. He would go to great lengths to assist in a good practical joke on some staff member and his hearty laughter was part of the general enjoyment. It was a long time before his staff knew that a form of diabetes had been troublesome to him for some years for he continued his heavy programme of organization and travel. He saw many of his plans for the Foresters bring new splendour each year, for he was an imaginative public relations man. He could even be a showman when occasion demanded. He once arranged to have more than a thousand new members initiated in a group at a mass meeting in Massey Hall in Toronto, and at the annual and well-known Canadian National Exhibition he made the marquee of the Foresters a popular meeting place by stocking it with writing supplies and other conveniences for public use.

The Doctor's greatest pleasure was to visit the various lodges and his visits were always great occasions for they all enjoyed doing him honour. These were his friends.

But it became apparent that his health was waning. His last public appearance was at a banquet at the Temple Building in 1906 during which some new staff members were introduced. A doctor advised against his attendance and everyone was shocked to see how ill he looked, but the great enthusiasm of their greeting made him very happy. It was soon after this that he left on another journey but this time it was in a search for health. He spent some weeks in Savannah, Georgia, and for a time he looked much better for the rest, but a sudden heart seizure brought death in November 1907.

At the time of his passing, newspapers across the land carried editorials, some of which would have brought forth that wonderful laughter. "He was a man of extraordinary parts. The stranger would take him for a high-class Englishman." This was one of the few attitudes that, for all his love for Oxford, made his eyes flash.

Toronto, his beloved city, mourned for this man who had brought honour to Canada. "The Mayor and aldermen, the members of his Executive Council, representatives of the High Courts and a guard of honour of Royal Foresters led the thousands who waited at the Union Station for his last return to Toronto. His casket was carried on the shoulders of eight Foresters to the waiting funeral carriage. Then was formed a procession, the like of which Toronto has not often looked upon, to escort this great man and illustrious Forester to Massey Hall. There Dr. Oronhyatekha's body was to lie in state. More thousands of citizens of every degree and all ranks lined the streets. The drawn blinds, the bared heads and the sorrowful faces formed a tribute of respect such as is paid to few men either in life or death." So said the newspapers of the time.

Memorial services were held in countless places across the continent on both sides of the border, and many people accompanied the special train that took him home to Deseronto to rest in the cemetery with his people.

Dr. Oronhyatekha, Peter Martin, was for twenty-six years the Supreme Chief Ranger of the Independent Order of Foresters, guiding its growth from a straggling bankrupt group in 1881 to a membership of thousands with an enormous reserve fund. He never enriched himself but in tributes from his fellow men he had great wealth. "In the early days," *The Forester* said, "Oronhyatekha was looked upon

157

as a visionary. Yet in his life he saw his cherished ideal of fraternity with insurance soundly established."

It was told later that on his death the only article found in his pocket was a poem written by his friend, Ernest Crosby, a New Yorker, social reformer, and writer, whose sentimental verse he had long enjoyed. These were the lines on the worn page:

> *So he died for his faith? That is fine—*
> *More than most of us do.*
> *But say, can you add to that line*
> *That he lived for it, too?*

INDEX